What People are Saying abo

M000189002

The biblical truth of holiness is made both practical and applicable in this compilation of teachings written by scholars, leaders, and pastors. Your life and ministry will be enriched as you discover how to take the profound reality of holiness and make it personally relevant!

Stephen E. Wilson
Senior Pastor
Greeley Wesleyan Church

A new era of missional holiness is dawning upon us. This transformational book is the manifesto. What a wonderful time to be Wesleyan!

Mark O. Wilson
Senior Pastor
Hayward Wesleyan Church

Holiness hits the streets. The authors remind us that God's grace results in changed lives that change the world.

John Bray
Senior Pastor
Heritage Church

We live in a time when our holiness has been shaken through the sieve of experiential failures and we have come to believe that true holiness does not exist. This inspirational book effectively lays the theological foundation with clarity and reveals true to life applications that make holiness come to back to life. Read, enjoy, apply, experience, and live it.

Joe W. Colaw
Senior Pastor
First Wesleyan Church

If you're tired of the generic, plug-n-play approach to developing transformed lives in your church, here is something you will love. These four holiness leaders bring their honest, practical, and straightforward wisdom to help you develop an infrastructure for holiness in your local church. What a great help to those of us trying to lead the people of God.

Steve DeNeff
Senior Pastor
College Wesleyan Church

Rarely does one resource have both breadth and depth, combined in a way so applicable for both an individual and a church. Be warned—you may well be transformed!

Wayne Schmidt
Senior Pastor
Kentwood Community Church

I sincerely believe that the Wesleyan holiness message, as presented in this resource, is tailor-made for our generation. The understanding that holiness begins in the heart but is designed to move from the heart to the hands, mouth, and feet of a Christ-follower, cries out to find its place in a world so obviously in need of a touch of God's love.

Karl Eastlack
Senior Pastor
Eastern Hills Wesleyan Church

One of the most practical books on holiness I have read. Once I began reading it, I couldn't put it down. I was inspired—a great reminder that it's not just about me. Holiness will move us outward to touch our families, our communities, our churches and this world for the glory of God. A must read book for anyone seeking to go deep in Christ.

Jim Lo
Dean of the Chapel
Indiana Wesleyan University

I believe God is giving the holiness movement another chance—raising up men and women who are calling us to be faithful to our heritage and the Word of God. This book contains the summons of four such leaders. I pray we'll listen and respond.

Stephen J. Lennox
Professor of Bible
Indiana Wesleyan University

Holiness for the Real World explores the rich biblical message of holiness that is *wholistic* in scope. Combined together, this challenging resource shows us how to spread hope and holiness that will transform our world.

Thomas E. Armiger
General Superintendent
The Wesleyan Church

HOLINESS
FOR THE REAL WORLD

CHRIS BOUNDS

JAMES GARLOW

CHRISTY LIPSCOMB

JO ANNE LYON

wesleyan
publishing
house

Indianapolis, Indiana

CONTENTS

FOREWORD

When the "holiness movement" disintegrated (as a movement) some thought that the doctrine and experience of entire sanctification would disappear. Holiness churches had moved on in recent decades to other issues like denominational programs, church growth, church planting, and leadership development. However, after several decades of neglect, Wesleyans are now rediscovering the doctrine and experience of holiness. The evidence of this growing rediscovery was apparent at the 2008 General Conference when the conference featured the Forum on Holiness with four major speakers presenting holiness in a fresh way.

These presentations did not give us a new doctrine of holiness, so much as lodge the experience of holiness in the current context of what the church should *be* and should be *doing*. After so many had tossed out the baby (holiness) with the bathwater (abusive ways of teaching on holiness), there is a new interest in recovering the baby to put in our fresh bathwater. The emphasis of the church is shifting, and these four speakers are willing to lodge these new emphases squarely in the doctrine of holiness—something we have failed to do with other recent emphases in the church.

This book still calls us to holiness as a personal experience for every Christian—whether by a shorter, middle, or longer way. But it also reminds us that holiness is more than a personal experience with God. A real dose of Christian holiness will produce a holy church that moves beyond itself to reform the world and care for the needy. These fresh emphases are not new but are squarely in the tradition of the early holiness movement.

To me the greatest encouragement to us all is that *holiness* and *entire sanctification* are terms we are again using. As you read this book may you be magnetically drawn to God's great reservoir of grace that is personal, corporate, and global. I pray that this will inspire you to seek God's sanctifying work for both yourself and your church and that it will rouse a host of Christians to get involved in bringing Christ's kingdom to pass—so that God's will is done on earth as it is in heaven.

Keith Drury

CHRIS BOUNDS

Dr. Chris Bounds serves as Associate Professor of Religion at Indiana Wesleyan University in Marion, Indiana. Prior to that, he served eight years as a pastor in Arkansas. Dr. Bounds earned a bachelor of arts degree in Bible and Greek at Asbury College, a master of divinity degree at Asbury Theological Seminary, and a Ph.D. in Theological and Religious Studies at Drew University, with an emphasis in Systematic and Wesleyan Theology. As a pastor, theologian, and professor, Dr. Bounds is passionately committed to proclaiming Wesleyan theological distinctives to his students, the Church, and society.

PERSONAL HOLINESS
Grace for Transformed Lives

CHRIS BOUNDS

Holiness unto the Lord is a phrase deeply rooted in The Wesleyan Church and the American holiness tradition. This phrase not only states what God requires of us, but points to a beautiful possibility and hope in the present life: God can make us holy.

The deepest longing of the human heart is to be fully God's. Within each of us is the desire to love God without reservation, to live in faithful obedience to Him, and to give ourselves in love and service to other people, just as Christ did. This is the human yearning for holiness.

What if our holiest longings could be realized right now? What if God would exchange our "bent toward sinning" for a natural propensity to love God and neighbor? Wouldn't we take advantage of it? The good news of Jesus Christ and the message of The Wesleyan Church is that God can set us free to love and walk as faithful disciples of Jesus Christ.

The Wesleyan Church's Doctrine of Holiness

Theologians call the process leading to personal holiness *sanctification*. The Holy Spirit is transforming our lives from the moment we are born again until we receive glorification in death. The Spirit's work is designed to restore the full image of God in us, making us like Christ.

The Spirit transforms our attitudes, interests, and actions, while confronting our internal drive toward selfishness and sin. This is often called *initial* and *progressive sanctification*. However, Wesleyans believe the Spirit in a decisive moment can (1) deliver us from this twisted internal drive, (2) free us to love God with our whole heart and our neighbor as ourselves, and (3) enable us to obey completely God's revealed will. This work of the Spirit has been called *Christian perfection*, *perfect love*, *Baptism of the Holy Spirit*, *entire sanctification*, and *fullness of the Spirit*. As we continue to submit to the Spirit, we are conformed more and more to the image of Christ until we reach *final sanctification* at the moment of glorification in death.

There are a variety of ways people have understood the process of sanctification, ranging from more to less optimistic. Specifically, we'll examine three Wesleyan-Arminian perspectives on entire sanctification plus a fourth from outside our tradition that has nevertheless had some influence.

The Shorter Way—Entire Sanctification Now

The most optimistic view, known as the *shorter way*, is that Christians can experience entire sanctification now by an act of consecration and faith: surrendering to the lordship of Christ and trusting God to sanctify. The Holy Spirit responds to such an act by

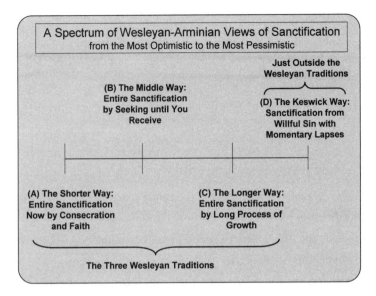

A Spectrum of Wesleyan-Arminian Views of Sanctification
from the Most Optimistic to the Most Pessimistic

Just Outside the
Wesleyan Traditions

(B) The Middle Way:
Entire Sanctification
by Seeking until You
Receive

(D) The Keswick Way:
Sanctification from
Willful Sin with
Momentary Lapses

(A) The Shorter Way:
Entire Sanctification
Now by Consecration
and Faith

(C) The Longer Way:
Entire Sanctification
by Long Process of
Growth

The Three Wesleyan Traditions

delivering the Christian from the power of sin and empowering him or her to walk in love of God and neighbor.

In this view, every believer has the power—as a gift of prevenient grace, regenerating grace, or as an uncorrupted part of free will—to do the human work required in entire sanctification. Because the Holy Spirit is always ready to respond to a personal act of consecration and faith, only ignorance, unwillingness, or unbelief can prevent the believer from experiencing entire sanctification.

There is a difference, however, between entire sanctification and Christian maturity. A person may be set free from sin, perfected in love, and empowered for ministry, without having the knowledge, wisdom, and experience necessary for Christian maturity. A believer can know what to do, but not have the power or proper motivation to do it in a way fitting with spiritual maturity. Yet a Christian cannot become fully mature without the experience of entire sanctification.

Primarily associated with the teaching of Phoebe Palmer and the American holiness movement, this position can be seen in Keith Drury's *Holiness for Ordinary People*[1] and Kenneth Grider's *A Wesleyan-Holiness* Theology.[2] It is the position expressed in the Articles of Religion of The Wesleyan Church[3] and thus the official teaching of The Wesleyan Church.

The Middle Way—Seeking until You Receive

The second view, known as the *middle way*, agrees that entire sanctification results from personal consecration and faith. It also agrees on the distinction between Christian maturity and holiness. However, this view denies that all believers inherently have the faith necessary for entire sanctification. Rather, sanctifying faith is a gift of grace given to believers as they seek God for entire sanctification in the means of grace—such as public worship, prayer, Bible reading, fasting, and Holy Communion.

> But you were washed, you were sanctified, you were justified in the name of the Lord Jesus Christ and by the Spirit of our God.
>
> 1 Corinthians 6:11

Christians are taught to actively seek entire sanctification, availing themselves of the various means of grace and waiting for God's grace to create the necessary faith to appropriate it. Thus, Christians cannot be entirely sanctified at any moment they choose, but only when God makes available the grace that can create such faith.

This view of entire sanctification is seen in Steve DeNeff's *Whatever Became of Holiness,*[4] in some of John Wesley's more optimistic pieces like "The Scripture Way of Salvation,"[5] and is a possible alternate interpretation of The Wesleyan Church's Articles of Religion.[6]

The *middle way* is often suggested in practical counsel—even by those who hold to the *shorter way*—when entire sanctification is not immediately realized despite a person's best efforts at consecration and faith. For example, Keith Drury advises Christians who don't immediately experience entire sanctification to continue to seek it through the various means of grace.

The Longer Way—A Long Process of Growth

The third perspective, often called the *longer way*, teaches that entire sanctification is most often realized after many years of spiritual development, a long journey of dying to self. Some Christians experience entire sanctification in this life, but most will not obtain it until just before death or at the point of death. This view emphasizes the persistence and stubbornness of original sin, a recalcitrance that is only overcome through gradual, significant growth in grace, personal denial, and spiritual development.

In this view, entire sanctification is described as a slow death to sin. It involves a long process, which is often painful and arduous, until death to sin eventually occurs. While this view does not deny the possibility of a short process and early death, or the exercise of personal faith in appropriating entire sanctification, its focus is on the long progression. The moment in which a Christian dies completely to self is always the goal, but the process leading to the goal is the primary focus. Many who adhere to this doctrine of holiness closely link entire sanctification with Christian maturity.

This view is described and embraced in Thomas Oden's *Life in the Spirit*,[7] in Randy Maddox's *Responsible Grace*,[8] and in John Wesley's more pessimistic writings, such as "Brief Thoughts on Christian Perfection."[9] While this has not been the dominant teaching in the American Holiness tradition, or the official teaching of The Wesleyan Church, it has been taught in various circles, and embraced by many.

The Keswick Way—Sanctification from Willful Sin

The Keswick teaching asserts that Christians can be free from *willful sin*, but cannot be completely delivered from *original sin* in this life. Instead, they will continue to struggle with rebellion, selfishness, and pride. This is more than external temptation, but an internal bent to sinning that persists throughout life. The believer can live above the sin nature in any given situation, but cannot be truly free from it.

A Spectrum of Wesleyan-Arminian Views of Sancification

(1) The "Shorter Way" Entire Sanctification Now by Consecration and faith	Key Points:	Examples:
	• Can be free from willful sin and original sin, not infirmity	Phoebe Palmer, Keith Drury, The Articles of Religion of The Wesleyan Church
	• Consecration and faith are inherent powers in Christians as a result of prevenient grace or conversion.	
	• Believers can experience entire sanctification any time they want. They decide where and when entire sanctification happens.	
	• Makes a distinction between entire sanctification and spiritual maturity	
(2) The "Middle Way" Entire Sanctification by Seeking until You Receive	**Key Points:**	**Examples:**
	• Can be free from willful sin and original sin, not infirmity	Steve DeNeff, the more optimistic John Wesley, The Wesleyan Church's Articles can be interpreted in this way. Often a default position when the "Shorter Way" does not bring a person into the experience of entire sanctification
	• Consecration and faith are not inherent powers in Christians.	
	• Believers can experience entire sanctification only when grace capable of creating sanctifying faith is made available.	
	• There is an element of God's timing. However, It happens sooner, rather than later.	
	• Makes distinction between entire sanctification and spiritual maturity	

(3) The "Longer Way" Entire Sanctification by Long Process of Growth	Key Points: • Can be free from willful sin and original sin, not infirmity • Believers can experience entire sanctification after long process of dying to self and spiritual development. • Few Christians will experience this depth of sanctification in this life • Entire sanctification and ultimate spiritual maturity are synonymous. Christian perfection is having the mind of Christ—saying and doing always what Christ would say and do.	Examples: Thomas Oden, Randy Maddox, the more pessimistic John Wesley, an unofficial position held by many in holiness denominations
(4) The "Keswick Way" Sanctification from Willful Sin with Momentary Lapses	Key Points: • Christians can be free from willful sin, but can not be liberated from original sin. There will always be the war between the "flesh" and "Spirit" • Willful sin is the exception rather than the norm in the Christian life • May happen in conversion or a second definite work of grace.	Examples: D. L. Moody, Robert McQuilkin, Bill Bright, Ian Thomas, an unofficial position held by many in holiness denominations

The Keswick perspective often has taught that willful sin is an exception rather than the norm of Christian life. Some forms of Keswick doctrine teach that victory over willful sin is given in conversion, while most forms emphasize a *second work of grace* experience. For those traditions which describe an experience subsequent to salvation, terms like *higher Christian life*, *deeper Christian life*, or *Spirit-filled life* are often used to talk about the life of holiness.

In many ways the Keswick position resembles the Wesleyan teaching, except for its view on the intractability of original sin. In the nineteenth and twentieth centuries there was significant interaction and cross pollination between Wesleyans and Keswicks. Both traditions were intimately involved in the American holiness movement. Therefore, while the Keswick view is not the official view of The Wesleyan Church, its teaching on holiness continues to exist in The Wesleyan Church among its preachers and laity.

The Wesleyan-Arminian view of holiness has been manifested historically in the shorter, middle, and longer ways, as well as interacting with Keswick teaching. The Wesleyan Church's Articles of Religion embrace the shorter way and can be interpreted as allowing a middle way, while clearly distinguishing themselves from the longer way and Keswick teaching.

The Wesleyan Church's Core Beliefs on Personal Holiness

There are five core Wesleyan teachings on personal holiness that give guidance for its experience in the present life.

Redemption from Inward and Outward Sin

The Wesleyan Church believes in personal redemption from inward and outward sin in the present life. Not only can Christians be liberated from willful sin, they can also be set free from the inner inclination to rebellion, selfishness, and pride and have their hearts oriented in love to God.

There have been a number of expressions used by Wesleyans to describe the inward freedom from the power of original sin.

Negatively, *eradication of the sin nature*, *overcoming the sin principle*, *cleansing from original sin*, and *deliverance from inward rebellion* have been some of the popular ways this work of sanctification has been described. Positively, *baptism of the Holy Spirit*, *infilling of the Spirit*, *perfect love*, *full salvation*, and *second blessing* have been some of the expressions used to define this work of sanctification. Regardless of the language used, all of these expressions convey a redemption from that part of human existence that sets itself up against the rule of the Holy Spirit in the Christian life.

> And we, who with unveiled faces all reflect the Lord's glory, are being transformed into his likeness with ever-increasing glory, which comes from the Lord, who is the Spirit.
>
> 2 Corinthians 3:18

However, the ultimate purpose of entire sanctification is not freedom from sin but *perfect love*—loving God with your heart, soul, mind, and strength and loving your neighbor as yourself. The inward sanctifying work of the Spirit removes the spiritual obstacles to the heart's orientation of love for God and neighbor.

Grace and the Means of Grace

Wesleyans emphasize grace as the basis for holiness. Entire sanctification is a gift of grace. It is not something we can generate, produce, or bring about in ourselves. It is God's work.

This raises the question, "How does God make saving and sanctifying grace available?" The Protestant tradition has emphasized the marks of the Church as the divinely appointed means of grace: preaching of the Gospel, receiving the sacraments, and participating in the Body of Christ through a local congregation. People cannot be spiritually regenerated, converted, and sanctified apart from these means.

From a Wesleyan perspective, the means of grace are vitally important because grace is essential to bring about spiritual transformation in attitudes, interests, and actions. Although Wesleyans have not always clearly delineated the means of God's grace, we have always taught that to the grace given in any moment, more grace must be given to progress in the way of salvation. The grace necessary for growth or progress and entire sanctification is made possible through the means of grace.

Entire Consecration and Faith

Personal consecration and faith are the means of appropriating entire sanctification. While there are differences among Wesleyan-Arminians about how to understand consecration and faith, all affirm the necessity of both as a means to entire sanctification.

While consecration is essential for entire sanctification, it is not the same thing. A truly Wesleyan view affirms that a Christian may be fully surrendered to the Lord and not entirely sanctified. A believer must still exercise faith in order to appropriate entire sanctification. However, a believer cannot be entirely sanctified without being fully surrendered to Christ.

> It is God's will that you should be sanctified.
>
> 1 Thessalonians 4:3

All of the views described above have been used by God to bring people to entire sanctification. However, one of the chief contributions of the holiness movement and the historic teaching of The Wesleyan Church has been the optimism in which it has affirmed that entire sanctification can truly be experienced sooner rather than much later. A Christian does not have to wait a lifetime to grow into entire sanctification.

Assurance of Entire Sanctification

At their best, each of the Wesleyan traditions has emphasized both a subjective and objective process for personal examination to see if entire sanctification has occurred. These traditions all have their roots in John Wesley, who provided practical advice for the discernment and verification of entire sanctification.[10]

The objective process is a self-examination of your heart and motives. Steve DeNeff provides an update of Wesley's questions: Is my conscience clear? Is my religion an obsession or a hobby? Do the people closest to me see this holiness in my life? Do I have power over sin? Do I have perfect love? Do I have genuine joy?[11] This objective inquiry is seen also in questions posed by Keith Drury: Have I made a total consecration to Christ? Do I have power over willful sin? Have I experienced a distinct increase in love for others? Is obedience the central focus of my life?[12] If Christians cannot honestly answer these questions positively, entire sanctification has probably not happened.

In the subjective form of verification, the Holy Spirit testifies to the believer's heart that entire sanctification has happened. A Christian may ask, "Do I have the witness of the Holy Spirit that I've experienced entire sanctification?" Just as a believer can have "an inward impression upon the soul" of being a child of God, he or she can have a similar witness to entire sanctification. However, it is possible for Christians to be entirely sanctified and not have the internal witness of the Spirit.

Thus, through this objective and subjective process, Wesleyans can help Christian seekers prayerfully discern whether entire sanctification has happened in their lives and assist them in progressing in the way of holiness.

Continued Temptation and Dependence upon Christ

The Wesleyan Church has consistently taught that there is no state of sanctification or depth of holiness in the present life that makes a believer immune from temptation. The ongoing struggle between the Spirit and the flesh can be broken in entire sanctification, but that does not mean that such believers are without any occasion for struggle. Being set free from the nature of sin does not set a person free from temptation or the possibility of being drawn to sin.

Believers are continually dependent upon God's grace for maintaining and walking in entire sanctification. John Wesley compared this constant dependency to a vine being connected to a branch. As long as the vine is grafted into the branch the nourishing sap continues to flow into the vine. However, if the vine is cut off from the branch, the vine withers and dies. In the same way a Christian must be connected continually to Christ, continually dependent upon Christ for the grace necessary to walk in holiness. Grace must be communicated to the believer and as such Christians must avail themselves of the means of grace.[13]

In addition, Wesleyans believe that Christians are not free from mistakes in judgment, from clouded understanding, or from ignorance. Thus, while Christians can have the right motivation behind their actions, the impetus of love, and be empowered to do God's will, because their understanding, judgment, and knowledge are impaired, they may still engage in misguided or incorrect decisions and actions. Entirely sanctified believers continue to fall short of God's perfection and need Christ's atoning work to apply to their infirmities, and seek forgiveness of wrongs committed out of infirmity against God and others. As such, there is the need for Wesleyans to pray daily the Lord's Prayer, and when they have offended another person, unintentional or not, they need to go and seek forgiveness and reconciliation.

In summary, while there has been some latitude of expression in the Wesleyan-Arminian tradition, there is an identifiable core of beliefs that have defined the Wesleyan-Arminian teaching on sanctification in general and The Wesleyan Church's doctrine in particular.

Spiritual Counsel On Experiencing Entire Sanctification

We have tried to lay a theological foundation in which to understand The Wesleyan Church's teaching on personal holiness. At this point, we want to begin to apply it practically to those among us who desire to experience the beauty and promise of holiness.

While the longer way is a part of the larger Wesleyan-Arminian tradition, and God has used it to bring people into greater depths of personal holiness, it can be discouraging. All too often it leads us to believe that we have to wait a lifetime before we can hope ever to be entirely sanctified. This leaves us with little expectation for this work of grace to be done in our foreseeable future and results in a lack of earnest seeking for this experience.

> You cannot study the Bible diligently and earnestly without being struck by an obvious fact—the whole matter of personal holiness is highly important to God!
>
> A.W. Tozer

The beauty of The Wesleyan Church's teaching is the optimism and expectation that God can work in the present moment to bring about entire sanctification. It fosters in Christians a posture of expectation and earnest seeking, confident that the holiest longings of the human heart can be realized in our lives, sooner rather than later.

Surrender Fully to Jesus Christ

If we desire to experience entire sanctification, we need to fully surrender our lives to Jesus Christ. We cannot hold back any part of our lives from God. We need to give it all to God—our dreams, talents, fears, emotional wounds, physical resources, strongholds of sin, divided heart, pride—and withhold nothing. We must be willing to go anywhere and do anything for God.

> Why are we not more holy? Chiefly because we are enthusiasts, looking for the end without the means.
>
> John Wesley

We must consecrate to God all areas of our lives over which we have control, as well as those over which we have no control—the beauty and ugliness of our lives. Christ must have it all. If we are unwilling or unable to do this, the possibility of entire sanctification for us is seriously handicapped and we need to seek Christ for his grace to enable us to make this total consecration.

Believe in the Divine Work of Entire Sanctification

If we desire to experience entire sanctification, we need to believe that Christ presently makes people holy in decisive moments. It is not enough for us to suppose theoretically that it is possible for God to bring about personal holiness; we must believe that God indeed does it in Christian hearts.

There is a deep and pervasive skepticism about entire sanctification in the American Church and cynical attitudes even among traditional Wesleyan Holiness denominations. There are at least three reasons for such disbelief. First, even though Evangelicalism talks about spiritual transformation in Christ, much greater focus is placed on justification and the forgiveness of sins. When sanctification is taught, it is portrayed as a slow and gradual process, rather than a sudden, decisive intervention of God. Second, many believers who grew up in the American Holiness tradition have sought entire sanctification. When they did not experience it after a time, they lost hope that it could be realized in the present moment. Finally, many doubt the possibility of entire sanctification because they witnessed such poor examples of holy living among those who professed the experience of entire sanctification.

If we desire personal holiness for our lives, but are skeptical about its attainability, we need to ask the Holy Spirit to give us "eyes to see" and "ears to hear" the truth of the doctrine and open our hearts to its possibility.

Ask Christ in Faith Specifically for Entire Sanctification Now

If we desire to enter into the experience of entire sanctification, we need to go to Christ in faith and specifically ask him to sanctify us entirely in the present moment. Because entire sanctification is the work of Christ made possible through his life, death, resurrection, and exaltation and through the outpouring of the Holy Spirit, it is not something we can generate, produce or bring about in ourselves. We are totally dependent upon God to do this miraculous work in our lives. Therefore, we must go to him and ask him for the gift of entire sanctification. While God can do the work of entire sanctification without specific intercession for it, he brings personal holiness most often in response to prayer. We need to call on the name of the Lord for it.

When we ask, we must exercise faith in Christ to bring personal holiness immediately into our lives. This faith in Christ is more than a general belief in the divine work of entire sanctification, the belief that God does this work in human lives; it is a personal faith in Christ that Christ desires to do this work *in our lives* and will do it now *in our lives*.

If we lack personal faith to believe God for entire sanctification in our lives, if God has not given us faith to believe, again we need to go to the Lord and ask for personal faith. John Wesley taught that sanctifying faith is a *divine conviction*. It is a gift of grace, a creation of the Holy Spirit in the human heart enabling Christians to believe God to sanctify them in the moment. The enduring scriptural prayer, "Lord, I believe, help my unbelief," is most appropriate here. We must ask the Lord for personal faith to believe that he can make us holy in a moment.

Seek Entire Sanctification Persistently until God Brings It

If entire sanctification does not happen in the moment we initially ask for it or even after a season, we need to persistently seek this experience and the faith that appropriates it in the means of grace, looking for the Holy Spirit to work through these means to bring personal holiness into our lives, and not grow weary until God brings it to us. While God is not limited to bringing entire sanctification only to those who persistently seek it, we most likely will miss out on this divine gift without such diligence and hunger. Entire sanctification by faith must be actively sought and not passively.

What does it mean to seek entire sanctification persistently until God brings it? Concretely, what does this look like? Although hardly exhaustive, here is a sketch of some of the ways we diligently seek for personal holiness in the means of grace. We regularly set aside specific time in our lives to fast and pray for the experience of entire sanctification. We find people who have experienced entire sanctification in their lives, listen to their testimonies and counsel, and ask for their intercession. We read and study holiness literature and biographies of Christians who lived lives of complete surrender to God. We seek out other Christians who believe in entire sanctification to lay hands on them and pray for this work of grace to be done in our lives. We seek to be a part of a group that keeps us accountable for persistently seeking entire sanctification until it happens. As we participate in Holy Communion, we ask God to sanctify us. When altar calls are given to invite people to experience entire sanctification, we go forward to pray. We take opportunity to serve others through our local church, particularly the least, the last, and the lost, asking God to perfect our hearts in love as we serve. As we worship and hear the Scriptures read and the Word of God proclaimed, we listen attentively for the still small voice of the Spirit to say to us, "Today is the day of your deliverance." When we hear about God moving in power in a particular church or in a particular place, as we are able, we go to seek the Lord there. Through actively seeking the experience of entire sanctification by faith in these and other means of grace, we position ourselves to receive God's sanctifying work when God by his grace brings it.

Conclusion

Toward the end of his life in an expression of mature thought, John Wesley wrote a sermon entitled "Causes for the Inefficacy of Christianity" in which he examined the reasons behind Christianity's ineffectiveness in eighteenth-century England. Wesley asked, "Why has Christianity done so little good in the world? Is it not the balm which the great Physician has given to men, to restore their spiritual health?" To which he replied, "I am bold to affirm, that those who bear the name of Christ are in general totally ignorant, both to the theory and practice of Christianity; so that they are perishing by thousands for lack of knowledge and experience . . . of justification by faith, the new birth, inward and outward holiness." Wesley makes clear in his sermon that if holiness is not preached, if it is not communicated, then it can't be experienced in human hearts and lives. To refrain from teaching about personal holiness in "theory and practice" is to withhold the "balm which the great Physician has given to men, to restore their spiritual health."[14] May we as The Wesleyan Church continue to be faithful in our proclamation of "Holiness unto the Lord" and may God continue to use it as a means of his grace bringing people into the experience of full salvation.[15]

Questions for Personal Reflection and Application

1. Consider your own experience with entire sanctification. Which of the four views presented in this chapter best resonates with you? What are the reasons? Which do you think is best supported by Scripture?

2. Five core Wesleyan teachings on holiness are listed. What do you think is the value of such a list? How might it help advance discussion about the doctrines of holiness and entire sanctification?

3. Where are you at in your experience with holiness? Which means of grace are you most consistently participating in? Which might deserve more attention? How might you incorporate the means of grace more fully into your life?

Personal Holiness: Grace for Transformed Lives

Executive Summary

The good news of Jesus Christ and The Wesleyan Church is that God can set us free to walk as faithful and holy disciples of Jesus Christ. Wesleyans believe that the Spirit can (1) deliver us from our internal drive to sin, (2) free us to love God and our neighbor as ourselves, and (3) enable us to obey completely God's revealed will. This is called *entire sanctification*.

Wesleyans have understood this moment of sanctification in a variety of ways. The *shorter way* says that Christians can experience entire sanctification immediately by an act of consecration and faith. The *middle way* says that Christians must pursue the faith necessary for entire sanctification through *means of grace*, such as listening to preaching, praying, Bible reading, fasting, and Holy Communion. The *longer way* teaches that entire sanctification is generally only realized after long years of spiritual development, a journey of dying to self. The *Keswick way* teaches that Christians can immediately be free from willful sin, but will always struggle with the internal drive to sin. The *shorter* and *middle ways* are consistent with The Wesleyan Church's official position, while the *longer* and *Keswick ways* are less compatible.

There are five core Wesleyan teachings on personal holiness: (1) personal redemption from inward and outward sin, (2) grace as an essential means for holiness, (3) consecration and faith as necessary for entire sanctification, (4) possibility of assurance of entire sanctification, and (5) continued temptation and the need for dependence on Christ.

Christians can pursue entire sanctification by surrendering to Christ, believing in his divine work, asking him specifically for the gift, and seeking it persistently until God brings it.

JAMES L. GARLOW

Dr. Jim Garlow has served as Senior Pastor of Skyline Wesleyan Church in La Mesa, California, since 1995. A best-selling author, communicator, and historian, his historical commentary called "The Garlow Perspective" is heard daily on nearly 650 radio stations nationwide. Dr. Garlow earned a master of divinity degree from Asbury Theological Seminary, a master of theology degree from Princeton Theological Seminary, and a Ph.D. in historical theology from Drew University. He recently appeared on Larry King Live and the Dr. Phil show because of his leadership in defending marriage through California Proposition 8.

CORPORATE HOLINESS
Grace to Transform Our Churches

JAMES L. GARLOW

Periodically, something happens in the life of the church that causes us to experience a common sense of elevated righteousness. By intention or by default, a church enters into an increased awareness of God's righteousness being lived out through the whole body.

Recently, Cliff Barrows, who for many years was Billy Graham's music and program director, asked my wife Carol and me to speak at the The Cove at Billy Graham Center in Asheville, North Carolina. What happened in our three days at The Cove impacted us significantly. Cliff is now age eighty-five. George Beverly Shea, who was a mainstay as a soloist at Graham crusades, is ninety-nine. John Ennis, the piano player who has been with them for forty years, was there, as well as George Hamilton IV, a member of the Grand Ole Opry who has traveled a great deal with the Graham crusade. At age seventy, he is the young one of the group. As we spent time with these four, we became aware that we were experiencing something that was quite profound.

We watched how these four men, who had shared sixty years of ministry, related to one another: how deferential they were, how affirming they were, how warm they were, and how dismissive they were of receiving any kind of compliments. Accolades just rolled off them, because they were so fixated on Christ.

I told Carol there is all-encompassing integrity among these people. We later began to think of it as *atmospheric holiness*—something beyond those four individuals that penetrates the atmosphere. It is not that they don't have clay feet. Of course, they do. But it was something pervasive among them that went way beyond individual aspects of their personal walks with Christ.

A number of years ago, I took our pastoral staff to Los Angeles to visit thirty-seven churches in three days. An interesting dynamic occurred each time we walked into the auditorium and waited for the pastor. Within a few moments of waiting, our staff would form a judgment about how long they wanted to be there. In some cases, even before the pastor arrived, they would say, "Can we make this one really quick?" Or they would say, "Wow, let's spend some time here!"

> I am the LORD your God; consecrate yourselves and be holy, because I am holy.
>
> Leviticus 11:44

There was something in the atmosphere. They could detect the presence or the absence of the Holy Spirit in the life stream of that church.

I want us to think about how we can cultivate that kind of atmospheric holiness. How do we elevate the experience of holiness corporately in the common life of a church?

My thesis is a simple one: If individuals are able to make choices that create an environment where God's grace is released in personal holiness, congregations can also make choices that create an environment in which God's grace is released in corporate or atmospheric holiness.

Here is a series of events, though not in chronological order, that significantly impacted the church I pastor, Skyline Wesleyan Church, in California. The events illustrate some of the conditions which I believe create an environment for God to do what he does best by his grace.

Brokenness

The first event I'll illustrate was not merely a choice as much as it was a situation we found ourselves in. It is the story of Skyline Church's building challenges from the mid 1980's to 2000, and especially the litigation related to the building from 2000 to 2006. I inherited a wonderful church from two exceptionally gifted and talented pastors—founding pastor Orval Butcher and leadership expert John Maxwell. They are phenomenal. The church, however, had significant building problems. The campus had been moved from Lemon Grove to a Rancho San Diego mountain location. It was extremely challenging, taking years and costing millions. Referring to the building complications, I jokingly say that I inherited a mess, but I managed to make it much messier.

Churches, like individuals, sometimes walk through very deep waters. Such painful and humiliating experiences, if we respond properly, can create an opportunity for God's grace to be poured out. It can place a church in a posture to be more vulnerable to receiving the thumbprint of Christ's righteousness.

Skyline's building problems lasted decades and were extremely distressful. When we moved in on April 15, 2000, we thought there would finally be a reprieve. Instead, we got mired in a massive lawsuit. Quite frankly, what I am about to describe is embarrassing to me, because it reflects in part on my leadership. Many pastors would have avoided some of the challenges we had. The bottom line is that because of the size of our facility and proximity to a major freeway, we were required by the state of California to widen the highway at a sum of nearly three million dollars. The man we hired to build the freeway and his subcontractors didn't follow state plans or specification. We didn't know this until we were making the last payment. Then we were sued. Our church board, functioning in a fiduciary role, was placed in the difficult situation of needing to counter-sue. The lawsuit mushroomed to fifty-two subcontractors and eighty insurance carriers and it cost us more than six years and 7.2 million dollars. It also cost us nearly one thousand church attenders and all our staff.

I wondered at times if we would ever get out of the lawsuit. Though I didn't articulate it to many people, I began to wonder if Skyline would actually survive. I wish I could tell you I handled it like a mighty man of faith, but I did not. I had horrific periods of crying out, sobbing, in the night hours when the pain was too great and only groaning would come out. I would recite Psalm 20:7 because that was the verse God gave me when he called me to the church almost thirteen years ago: "Some trust in chariots and some in horses, but we trust in the name of the LORD our God." I would say, "Oh, Jesus, oh, Jesus," and I would hear the voice of God say, "You are saying the right word. You are saying the only word you can say right now."

Positively though, in the midst of this, God was doing something to me internally, and to us as a church. He began to strip from me the sense that my identity had to be tied to attendance or any other external factor. I began moving toward the place God had wanted me to be for years—to where I was finding my identity at the foot of the cross, rather than in a Monday morning report. In all candor, I'm not sure I fully made that trip, but I have traveled many, many miles toward that end and learned to hear the internal affirmation of a heavenly Father who says, "Well done, my son. I'm proud of you."

For many months and years, our pastors, church board, lay leaders, and entire congregation felt beat down, like we simply could not stop the process year after year. We thought at one point we finally had hit bottom: we had won a significant lawsuit with a concrete company that had cheated us out of massive amounts of concrete. It was unpleasant, but we were victorious and received a settlement. Two years later, a judge reviewed our case and found that our attorney failed to send a single correct notification. The judge overturned everything on this one technicality. We had to return everything plus cover court costs, attorneys' fees, everything. It cost us an enormous amount of money. The lawsuit—costing millions of dollars and years of time—is over. God saw us through it.

> For you are a people holy to the LORD your God. The LORD your God has chosen you out of all the peoples on the face of the earth to be his people, his treasured possession.
>
> Deuteronomy 7:6

There's much more to the story, but the point I want make is this: Though we certainly couldn't see it while we were in the midst of the mess, looking back, we can see it made us stronger. It made us much less boastful. I am not grateful for what we went through, but it has made me grateful now for every good moment we have in the life of the church. I'm not suggesting that being beat down innately produces corporate holiness. But I do believe that when you are beat down in the life of a local church, your attitude can create the environment in which the grace of Christ Jesus can come. Something in the brokenness of the human heart creates an avenue for

God to release his grace and the church is brought to a higher level. I like what I see spiritually in Skyline right now. I like the things that have been torn away, the fact that they are gone. I didn't like the process, but I love what's happening.

Look at your church; you have your own stories, your own journeys. They aren't identical to ours. It may not involve buildings or lawsuits, but you've gone through some hard times. If we look back on them and approach them with the right attitude, not grousing or complaining, but saying, "Okay, God, we're here for You," we find he does something in us when we come out of it; and we are stronger in the sense of community holiness.

Clinging to God

A second situation that promotes corporate holiness is illustrated by a recent petition drive to amend the constitution of the state of California. You might say, "What's that got to do with corporate holiness?" The answer is "A lot." In March 2000, California Proposition 22 was passed by 61.4 percent of voters affirming that marriage be recognized as the union between one man and one woman. Unfortunately, the mayor of San Francisco violated that and began to marry gay couples. As a result, Proposition 22 was contested under the Supreme Court of California. On May 15, 2008, four judges in California ruled that Proposition 22 is unconstitutional and that homosexuals must now be allowed to marry.

> May God himself, the God of peace, sanctify you through and through. May your whole spirit, soul and body be kept blameless at the coming of our Lord Jesus Christ. The one who calls you is faithful and he will do it.
>
> 1 Thessalonians 5:23–24

Pastors galvanized across the state and began working to collect enough signatures to put on the November ballot an amendment to the state constitution that declares marriage is between one man and one woman. If such an amendment could be passed, judges hopefully could not rule it unconstitutional, as they did with Proposition 22. It would be part of the constitution. Pushing hard, we achieved that goal, and the result is that an amendment will be on the November ballot.[1] Consequently, we requested a stay be granted. We asked that the state not allow people to marry whose marriages could later be declared illegal. But on June 4, the same four judges who overturned Proposition 22 said they would not grant the stay. So as of June 16, 2008, homosexuals can legally marry in the state of California.

Be aware too, that this issue is not limited to the state of California. When they approved a similar measure in Massachusetts, there was a technicality in the law that prevented it from coming to other states, but not so in California. They are calling it *marriage tourism*. People from all over the United States can fly to California to get married legally, and then fly back to their home states. Now, they are attempting to coerce other states to accept this new definition of marriage.

Let me be candid about what this has to do with corporate holiness for all of us. One politician said it this way, "We should fire, fine, and jail those who believe in traditional marriage until they relent." The bottom line is this. We are far more vulnerable as Bible believing people than we have ever been. Pastors are openly talking about how long it might be before the first one of us actually goes to jail for refusing to hire a practicing homosexual or refusing to marry homosexuals.

In other words, this has knocked props out from under us, and it's causing us to have a healthy clinginess to God. It is causing me to think differently, in the organizing and orchestrating of my life, what my future may hold. We are entering into a new season. If we approach this season correctly, it puts us in a great posture for receiving God's grace. His corporate holiness can be released in the church of Jesus Christ in America, in our local churches, in a way we have never known.

Desperation

In the midst of all this pressure coming upon us in California related to Proposition 22, I put a call into a friend of mine, Lou Engle. It was a call to come and teach us how to pray and fast. We were doing all the right things organizationally, but I could tell we were missing the prayer underpinnings. What I want to highlight for you is the impact of a forty day fast called out of a sense of high desperation. It is amazing what desperate people will do. It is one thing to call a fast; it is something else when you are very desperate.

In late 2002, a number of us pastors in San Diego got a call from the evangelist Franklin Graham. "I know you want to have my father for a Billy Graham crusade, but if you are going to have him, you are going to have to prepare for him in four months."

We said, "Four months?" This is the first of December in 2002.

He said, "Because of his health, you have four months to prepare for him, if you want him."

We said, "We'll do it."

And we did what most cities have taken two years to do. Four months later, we had an awesome Billy Graham crusade. Various people asked how we did it and my answer was quite simple. We were very desperate.

In support of the proposed constitutional amendment, I called Lou Engle and asked him to bring his forces in. As a result, we called the state of California to a forty day fast from September 24 to November 2, ending with thousands of people in San Diego's Qualcomm Stadium, fasting and praying and crying out for God.[2]

Even as all of this has sobered us a great deal, something good and wonderful is happening. There is a name for it. We call it corporate holiness.

Confessing Our Faith

Another thing we've done that I believe has prepared us to receive the grace of corporate holiness is that we began as a church to declare the Apostle's Creed every Sunday. I'm not one who is inclined toward this type of thing. However, I said we are not going to *recite* it; we are going to *declare* it. There is something powerful about a congregation vigorously declaring the Apostle's Creed. I said, "I want you to declare it, not recite it. These are words we live by and words for which we are willing to die. When you are ready to embrace what I've just said, you start saying it." The sound of people saying, "Not merely words that we live by, but words that we die for," began to raise the bar of excellence spiritually in our congregation.

> An unholy church! It is useless to the world, and of no esteem among men. It is an abomination, hell's laughter, heaven's abhorrence. The worst evils which have ever come upon the world have been brought upon her by an unholy church.
>
> C.H. Spurgeon

Communion

We also began to have communion every week for many months. I don't personally prefer a standardized liturgy. I'm one of those who (and I admit this is a weakness rather than a strength) see the word *liturgy* as meaning stodgy, dry, and sort of boring. Technically, the term *liturgy* only means a customary pattern of observance in public worship, but nonetheless the word to me has always smacked of something that lacks life rather than calling out vibrancy of life. So I had a particular resistance to Eucharistically-based services where I felt that there wasn't enough dynamic challenge for life change.

> Nothing can be more cruel than the leniency which abandons others to their sins. Nothing can be more compassionate than the severe reprimand which calls another Christian in one's community back from the path of sin.
>
> Dietrich Bonhoeffer

Nevertheless, I decided that we would simply do it, experience the Eucharist together every week for a time. But instead of focusing so much on personal preparation, the *subjective* aspect of the Lord's Supper, we're focusing more on the *objective* aspect, which is: ready or not, Christ is there. Of course, we want you to prepare and be ready for Communion—the scripture warns us not to come slovenly—but even more, we want you to be keenly aware of Christ's presence.

I have not tried to explain Christ's presence in the Lord's Supper; I don't want to rob people of the sense of mystery. Instead I said, "I cannot explain it, but Jesus is here in this event in a profound way." I began to watch and that objective emphasis brought a much greater sense of sobriety, a much greater sense of expectation.

Simplicity

Another way to promote corporate holiness is through simplicity. *Simplify* was a major theme in our church for about five months. Let me explain why this is important to corporate holiness. Keith Drury has correctly said that baby boomers have created churches they cannot sustain. They are too complex. So we find ourselves needing to simplify church structure. From September through December 2007 our pastoral staff met repeatedly wrestling with how to focus and harness our energies. We had a scattered approach to ministry and we were making the lives of our people far too complex. So the word *simplify* became the hallmark of the pastoral staff for the last half of 2007.

Then in January 2008, I said to the congregation, "How many of you feel that life is too complex, too difficult, too hard to live? Raise your hand." Every hand went up. We began to talk over the course of the next five months about how things in our lives can suffocate us, suffocate our spirits, and keep us from seeking the kingdom of God. So I said, "How many of you have too many things? You know you should throw a lot of it away." Every hand went up, so I said, "I'm going to test you. Eight days from now we are going to have a dumpster here on campus. You bring it, you dump here." Just to be safe, we brought in four dumpsters. We quickly had to bring a fifth, sixth, seventh, eighth—we ended up with seventeen massive dumpsters. People kept bringing stuff, not just from cleaning their garages, but out of a sense that they had allowed things to choke off Jesus' life within them.

Then we began to talk about a theology of simplicity. We talked about the Quakers and the Shakers. We went back to the early Holiness Movement and focused on what they taught about the relationship between holiness and simplicity.

We've also talked a lot about sharing. I said, "How many things are in your home that you ought to be sharing with somebody else? You're not giving it away, and you need to give it away. We are going to have an Acts 2:44 experience. We are going to have an *un-garage un-sale*. I want you to bring it to the church. It's not going to be sold, people are going to come to the church and pick up what they want." Now at first it looked like a disaster, but the ladies of the church who love garage sales went to work and they organized everything. It ended up being about a block or so long. It was a massive, joyous time of sharing.

Don Dayton, in his book *In Discovering an Evangelical Heritage*,[3] said that social reform flows from a life of holiness, because when grace is received, grace is given to others. When we share with one another, when we have an Acts 2:44 experience, we make ourselves vulnerable to receiving the thumbprint of Christ in the sense of corporate holiness.

Suffering

This final thing I want to share is still a very sensitive area for me. In June 2007, my wife was diagnosed with cancer. During those earliest days there were challenging times when I was driven to my hands and knees. Carol was so nauseous, the vomiting so persistent, her weight was plummeting and the doctors could not get it stopped no matter what they tried. Down on my hands and knees, cleaning up a terrible mess, I was groaning to God, saying to him, "God this isn't fair. Such and such a pastor is getting to do this, such and such a pastor is getting to do that." And I heard so clearly the voice of the Father saying, "This is the best ministry you have ever had. You are at this moment most like Jesus." I never complained again.

Several months later, I had to go through what I call the "knot-hole." It's when you know you have to fight for the life of your spouse, even though it seems to be failing. So you are fighting tena-ciously, vigorously hanging on, but then you realize that there is something fleshly about the way you are fighting, and you realize you have to honor your marriage vows. For us, it was: "We'll be with each other *until one of us places the other in the arms of God.*" So I came to that point where I knew that to fight with a fresh, spirit-given vigor, I had to release *my* way of fighting. I had to let her go and say, "Okay, God if she goes, she goes. And I will love You forever." In that release, I began to cooperate with the Holy Spirit, to partner with a God who understood and cared way more about Carol than even I do.

> The neglect of prayer is a grand hindrance to holiness.
> John Wesley

Suffering is remarkably unpleasant, but it has some wonderfully serendipitous side effects. For example, my passion for God devel-oped. My love for my wife escalated enormously. If we approach and embrace properly moments of suffering, it can result in an increased sense of holiness. Not just in the individual, but in the entire church family. This is why I suppose we call it, *good* grief. I don't suggest that Carol's illness was from God. Pain, suffering, heartache, sickness, disease, tears, and death all come from the hand of the enemy. However, in the midst of what the enemy can do in this broken world is Christ's indescribable presence. In that moment, we become most vulnerable to God's grace.

Through this experience, I began to blog. I am still too close to these events emotionally to sort them all out theologically. All I can say is that something began to happen to our church, some-thing in the inner core of who we are. Our DNA was altered.

One lady said to me, "I have been hearing reports of how you have been changed by this."

I said, "Well the real report is how the church has been impacted and changed by this; how they have changed in some awesome ways."

The church saw me in some of my most decimated moments, but I saw the Church in its best moments. I felt the presence of Jesus with me. It is in those moments we become so vulnerable to the presence of God that it stirs a deepening that we might call holiness.[4]

Conclusion

One day I was sitting with Dennis Kinlaw, one of the best communicators of the reality of the Old Testament I've ever known. He asked me, "When we taught about marriage, what is the real marriage—marriage here on earth or marriage as the culmination of history?"

Long pause, a tiny giggle, and he just looked at me. When Dennis Kinlaw looks at you, he looks at you in such a way that it makes you want to confess any sin you have ever thought of doing. He has that look. And he paused so long that I felt uncomfortable and needed to respond. I responded prematurely and consequently stupidly.

I said, "Oh, the marriage here on earth. God has borrowed the metaphor in a profound way so we can grasp what is going to happen in the marriage of the Lamb." I got about that far and I could tell by his look that I had answered wrongly. I stopped and brought my hands slowly back down.

I said, "You mean the real marriage is in Heaven?"

He said, "Yes."

"If that is the case, we have never seen a real marriage."

He said, "That is right."

I said, "Wow, we've never seen a real marriage; the real marriage is yet to happen. So our marriages here are only the shadows. We are only the *hors d'oeuvre*. We are only vibrant living metaphors of the real thing that is yet to come. The best marriage you can think of here on earth, no matter how good it is, it is only a metaphor of the ultimate marriage that is yet to come."

If that is true, and it is, then all of history is moving towards one grand climax. The Father has one kid, his boy, who is going to get married. Now, you care about anybody who gets married, but if you only have one boy, you are going to care about the bride. You are going to care that the bride is ready to marry your son. So the Father cares deeply about the bride he is cultivating right now to marry his only son, Jesus. He wants us to be so prepared for that moment.

God says, "I only have one boy and I want him to marry well. I want him to marry a bride that is not wrinkled, or spotted; someone who has saved herself." So what I have been sharing with you is not some extraneous sub-point in a systematic theology textbook. Corporate or community holiness is the very reason for which God made you, us, the Church. This is not extraneous. It is the epicenter of God's heart.

Questions for Personal Reflection and Application

1. What thoughts, if any, did you have about corporate holiness before reading this chapter? Do you think that you've experienced corporate or atmospheric holiness in the past?

2. How do you feel about the statement that congregations are able to make decisions that can help create an environment where God's grace is released for corporate holiness? Which of the conditions described are most important? Which are the most challenging?

3. What are two or three concepts or principles that you will take away from this chapter that could make a difference in your life and the life of your congregation?

Corporate Holiness: Grace to Transform Our Churches

Executive Summary

Congregations can pursue corporate holiness by embracing the conditions that help create an environment in which God's grace is released.

Brokenness. When hearts are broken, God responds with his grace. When the hearts of an entire congregation are broken, an avenue is opened for God's grace to create corporate holiness.

Clinging to God. Some circumstances cause us to cling to God. A congregation that clings to God is in an excellent posture for receiving God's grace of atmospheric holiness.

Desperation. Congregations that cry out in desperation to God provide an opportunity for God's Spirit to create a corporate sense of holiness.

Confessing our Faith. There is something powerful about a congregation confidently and faithfully proclaiming it's faith in God together. Such authentic declaration of belief prepares the congregation for the grace of atmospheric holiness.

Communion. What better way to raise the bar of holiness in a congregation than to regularly participate in the sacrament of Holy Communion, maintaining a keen awareness of Christ's presence.

Simplicity. Sometimes we allow our lives to become so complex that we choke off the life of Jesus within us. Simplicity is another way to promote corporate holiness.

Suffering. People who are suffering often have a greater sense of the presence of Jesus in their lives. This can be true of congregations as well as individuals.

God is preparing the bride—the church—to marry his only son, Jesus. You can be sure that he is deeply concerned about corporate holiness.

CHRISTY LIPSCOMB

Rev. Christy Lipscomb is the founding co-pastor of City Life Church, an inner-city, multi-cultural Wesleyan church in downtown Grand Rapids, Michigan. She is a graduate of Indiana Wesleyan University, earned a master of divinity degree at Asbury Theological Seminary, and is an ordained minister in The Wesleyan Church. City Life Church is a cross section of ethnicities, cultures, and economic levels.

MISSIONAL HOLINESS
Grace to Transform Our Communities

CHRISTY LIPSCOMB

I love the smell of possible redemption.

What does your community smell like? My church smells. I'm not talking fragrant offering or pleasing aroma. It's the smell of raw humanity. There is the smell of Michael, the homeless man, who rarely showers. There's the breath of Alice who came to church drunk a few weeks ago. Most Sundays there's the smell of cigarette smoke wafting in the back door as smokers satisfy their nicotine habits before morning worship. I love this . . . not because I enjoy cigarette smoke or the smell of perspiration, but because it reminds me that we are a broken, dirty, messed up, odorous group of people gathered together to find Jesus.

I have the privilege of being a pastor of an inner city church. About one-third to one-half of the people in our church are in rehab programs for drug and alcohol abuse. About one-quarter of the church are low-income families who live precarious lives—always on the edge of emotional breakdown, financial breakdown, or other types of extreme stress. Then there are a number of stable, middle class individuals and families who have felt moved to participate in this kind of ministry. We have more single people than married people in our church. We have more men than women. We are multi-ethnic, with Caucasians, African-Americans, and Latinos, and there are more felons than I care to know about. I often lose track of who has gone to jail for what.

This is my Samaria. Jesus tells us to go to Jerusalem, Judea, Samaria, and the far parts of the earth (Acts 1:8). The "far parts" are the places where people have completely different languages, different food, and different cultures. The Jerusalems and Judeas are where I find my own people, my own food, and my own language. Then there are the Samarias.

Samaria, as we know it in the New Testament, was born in a violent, turbulent time, in the throes of war. In 722 B.C., the Assyrian mega power swooped over the Northern Kingdom of Israel and carried off nearly thirty thousand people from Samaria. Many Assyrians were then transplanted from their homeland to repopulate Samaria. The new inhabitants worshiped pagan gods, and as time went on, they intermarried with the Samaritan Jews remaining in the land. A mish-mashed, syncretistic worship of the Lord and pagan gods emerged.

Years later, when the exiled Jews returned home, they had nothing but contempt for the half-breed Samaritans, because the Samaritans had not been able to maintain social holiness at the time it mattered most.

Samaria became the place to avoid—the out group, the *other*, the unfaithful, the unholy, the un-kosher, the impure outsider. Samaritan culture was distasteful, its morals questionable. Samaritan worship practices were disgraceful; they didn't even worship in Jerusalem. In other words, Samaria smelled.

Samaritans were never a significant *threat* to the Jews. They were more of an annoyance, an inconvenience. There was an old saying of the time: "Better to eat swine than Samaritan bread." Quite simply, Jews just preferred not to associate with Samaritans. And it was this reasoning that made Jesus' decision to travel through Samaria—where he would meet with the woman at the well—so very remarkable.

We tend to skip Samaria don't we? It's a natural tendency. Give a high school student a choice to do missions work overseas in some exotic country or in Samaria. Chances are Samaria is going to be second choice. Yet we're commissioned to go to the Samarias of this world.

> Therefore, I urge you, brothers, in view of God's mercy, to offer your bodies as living sacrifices, holy and pleasing to God—this is your spiritual act of worship.
>
> Romans 12:1

Like it or not, following Jesus means going to these undesirable places. What exactly are we to do once we're there? Every time Jesus sends his disciples out to do ministry, he gives them instructions to do three things. And it might not be the three things you'd first think of. Over and over he says to: preach the gospel, heal the sick, and cast out demons (Matt. 4:21–24; 9:32–35; 10:1, 7–8; 11:1–6; Mark 1:38–39; 3:13–15; 6:12–13; 16:14–20; Luke 4:17–21; 7:22; 9:1–2). As the sent-out church, we are *commanded* by Christ to go to Samaria, preaching, healing, and casting out demons.

Preaching in Samaria

First, we're to preach in Samaria. Preaching sounds like a safe, religious thing to do, right? Healing and casting out demons sound so supernaturally charged, but preaching? It's the safe one for normal Christians. But we have too low a view of preaching. In reality, preaching is to be a powerful, Holy Spirit-empowered work. Preaching is to be a supernatural act that counters opposition. It is to be a demonstration of the Spirit's power—an act of worship that is a stench to demons as much as it is a fragrant aroma to the Lord.

So what does preaching in Samaria look like? Social-holiness preaching speaks to society's evils. It addresses taboo topics that are sometimes uncomfortable to talk about in church. Most times the Apostle Paul mentions "principalities and powers," he is talking about socio-political structures, such as government or culture. He's talking about Rome. Paul recognizes the spiritual powers at work, but he typically describes them as being manifested at a societal level. They are personal forces with a systemic face; demons in the very structure of society. Social-holiness preaching addresses these forces at a systemic level for God's kingdom.

> But you will receive power when the Holy Spirit comes on you; and you will be my witnesses in Jerusalem, and in all Judea, and Samaria, and to the ends of the earth.
>
> Acts 1:8

Social holiness is a dance between confrontation and grace. We confront the principalities and powers with courage. We preach about taboo topics like sex, AIDS, homosexuality, divorce, addiction, polygamy, and immigration. We do this because the enemy loves to keep the church silent on these topics. The enemy loves for us to value niceness above holiness. But Jesus has come to set people *free*! Our speaking out of the silence opens doors. This holy confrontation takes courage. If you do not sometimes find yourself nervous to preach a message that the Holy Spirit has given you, I question whether your preaching is supernaturally powerful.

It takes great courage to preach the confrontational message of social holiness. But it also takes great grace. Jesus gives us a wonderful picture of this in his conversation with the woman at the well, when he brings up the subject of her marital status (John 4). Jesus tells her to go and call her husband. This brings up a world of confusion for the woman. Shame creeps up, and her intrigue with Jesus is immediately overshadowed by her desire to escape the embarrassing moment ahead. "Go, call your husband," Jesus tells her. As she stumbles for words to describe her six failed relationships, the woman finds it easiest to simply say, "I have no husband."

Look how Jesus handles this. He says, "You are right when you say you have no husband. The fact is, you have had five husbands, and the man you now have is not your husband . . ." (John 4:16–18). We might read this and think, "You tell her, Jesus! Lay down the law with this woman!" But Jesus is not condemning. Jesus knows the culture. Jesus knows Samaria. He knows that divorce was a male prerogative—women couldn't initiate it. He knows that marriage was a woman's security. No husband? That means no home, no food, and no future for women. He knows there is no logical reason that a woman would choose to be in her situation. It seems that this woman may have been passed from one man to the next, used up, and then passed on again. The men in the town divorced her. She didn't seek divorce. Jesus knows this, and he speaks the truth that Samaritan society has tried so hard to avoid mentioning. In effect, Jesus says with great gentleness, "Woman, I see what a terrible mess you're in." His acknowledgement of her pain is the key that unlocks her chains of bondage and sets her free.

Our preaching must confront the social evil. It must bring up the uncomfortable subject. And then it must relate to the individual with the tenderness of the Savior. Too often when we preach to Samaria—if we preach to Samaria—we speak the words that bring shame but fail to offer the words of living water that restore dignity and hope. It is easy to point out a lack of holiness; it is more difficult to gesture towards the path that leads to redemption.

My church is located on the street in our city that is infamous for prostitution. My city has an unofficial containment policy which means that within certain parts of town, the police turn a blind eye to prostitution or drug trafficking. Prostitutes will be arrested in the better parts of town, but they are much less likely to be arrested in the part of town where my church is located. It's all very unofficial, but no less real because of it. This is a societal evil. The powers and principalities are at work.

Mary was the name of one of the prostitutes on the corner outside our church. I first met her one Sunday morning before service when I invited her in for a cup of coffee. She looked at me with great suspicion and said in her raspy smoker's voice, "You know what I'm doing here, right? You're not stupid are you?"

I replied, "I know what you're doing. I just thought you'd like some coffee."

I left, and to my great surprise, about half an hour later, Mary came into the church. She only stayed a few minutes, but as time went on, everybody met Mary. She would come in for coffee and refreshments before church and several people would call out by name, "Hi, Mary!" She thrived on the attention and started to attend parts of the worship service.

Several months later, Mary was arrested for drug possession. I went to visit her in jail. As we chatted in the visitors' room, we talked about her lifestyle and her developing relationship with God. I shared with her the story of the prophet Hosea and his prostitute wife, and I told Mary how it showed that God loved her and would never give up on her. She had never heard that story before.

I preach many Sunday mornings, but there was something about sitting in jail with Mary and retelling that old story about Hosea and Gomer that felt like I was preaching on a truly important, supernatural level, probing and pushing against the devil's chains.

Jesus has sent us to *preach* to Samaria. We need Holy Spirit power to relate to Samaria. We need Holy Spirit-infused good news for our society's oppressed. Are you preaching to Samaria? Or are you tempted, like most of us, to skip it?

Healing in Samaria

The second reason Jesus sends us to Samaria is to heal. Now, Wesleyans from other parts of the world may have a different experience, but speaking for North America, healing is not a regular activity for most Wesleyans. And yet, it's one of three things Jesus repeatedly sends his disciples out to do.

> There is no holiness but social holiness.
>
> John Wesley

The word *salvation* in Greek is *sōdzo*, meaning to save, rescue, heal, cure, or restore to health. When we practice social holiness and take the gospel to our communities, we are not only introducing people to the giver of eternal life; we are introducing people to the Healer, Jesus Christ. Salvation is to be more than a ticket to heaven. Salvation is an introduction to a whole new life.

John Wesley had an abiding fascination with physical health. (And, for the sake of this discussion, I will limit the topic of healing to physical healing.) Wesley's medical guide, titled, *Primitive Physik: Or, an Easy and Natural Method for Curing Most Diseases*, was originally written anonymously. Wesley noted that most medical care was available only to the wealthy. He wrote this book as a practical guide for workers and others who couldn't afford doctors.

Wesley himself healed a woman with severe "head pain."[1] He also recounts a story in his *Journal* of his friend, Mr. Meyrick, who became ill and comatose. When Wesley went to check on him, Mr. Meyrick's pulse was gone. Wesley and several friends immediately prayed, and before their prayer was over, Mr. Meyrick's speech and sense had returned.[2] Wesley's beliefs on healing can perhaps be summed up best by this statement: "Let us examine the gift of healing. I have frequently said that it is not a sin to be sick or to die. It is, however, a sin for sickness and death to go unchallenged because there is no one to pray."[3]

As we consider social holiness, I doubt that healing is at the forefront of most of our minds. And yet, I cannot escape from the prominent role that it plays in Jesus' personal ministry and in his commissions to us.

> You are not here in the world for yourself. You have been sent here for others. The world is waiting for you!
>
> Catherine Booth

What are the sicknesses of our Samarias? Some of us have Samarias where people die from contaminated water. Some have Samarias near toxic waste dumps. A friend of mine came from a city near a toxic waste dump. A high majority of people in her town have cancer—way beyond the national average. She just expects to have cancer someday. Does the Lord care about these things? I think so.

I live as an ethnic minority in my African-American community. Traditional African-American food is called *soul food*. The history of soul food is both fascinating and disturbing. When slavery was legal in the United States, slaves were given scraps of food from slave owners' kitchens, including the less desirable pieces of meat. The slaves made do with what they were given. Foods like chitlins (intestines) and turkey knuckles are still popular in traditional soul food.

Do turkey knuckles and theology go together? I believe so. The U.S. has a history of social injustice with slavery. Generations later, we have an entire ethnic food tradition that continues to foster poor nutrition and bad health—a remnant of past social injustice. God cares about this stuff.

God created us as embodied people: spiritual, emotional, mental, and, yes—physical. The Word himself came to earth in flesh and blood—not only as a spiritual presence. When Jesus returns, his people will resurrect as embodied people. Our physical being is God's design. When we neglect to bring good news of healing to Samaria, we leave out one of Jesus' most dynamic messages of salvation.

Social holiness speaks to poor nutrition and hunger. Social holiness speaks to contaminated water. Social holiness speaks to toxic nuclear waste. When we quarantine ourselves from these things, we quarantine ourselves from the wrong things.

Jack is a white man in his thirties from rural Kentucky. He has a felony history because one time when he was drunk he burned down an apartment complex. Shortly after he was released from jail, Jack found our church. Today the man who burned down a building is, ironically, the leader of our church facilities.

Then there's Matthew. Matthew is a middle-aged black man. He's a single dad with three teenage kids. Matthew has diabetes and goes for kidney dialysis several times a week. He struggles to walk and has braces on both feet and uses a cane. He never complains, but physical life for this military veteran is challenging. He needs a new kidney.

Now here is a picture of healing on several levels: Jack recently had himself tested and learned he was a match to donate to Matthew. This former felon offered his kidney to Matthew.

Now, I don't know exactly all that Jesus had in mind when he told us to go to Samaria preaching, healing, and casting out demons, but I think Jack's offer might be one picture of what healing is like in God's kingdom. It's the physical healing, the healing of Jack's racism, the Body of Christ being united together.

Social holiness looks for ways we can be agents of healing in this diseased, sin-sick world. Social holiness sees healing as part of God's salvation message for his tainted creation. Transforming our communities requires that we look for ways to heal. Are you looking for ways to heal? Not only to heal yourselves and your Jerusalem, but are you looking for ways to heal Samaria? Or are you skipping Samaria?

Casting Out Demons from Samaria

We preach. We heal. And Jesus has also sent us to cast out demons. First, let's look at two extremes, which I'll very loosely call *literalist* and *liberal*. Literalists have an overly spiritualistic view of demonic work. They tend to neglect taking personal responsibility for what happens. When something goes wrong, "the devil is at work." *Liberals* on the other hand, talk about evil in generic, non-personal ways. The message comes across that if we're just nice enough people, we can end global war and poverty.

Neither extreme is especially helpful for social holiness. Literalists have power but no responsibility. Liberals have responsibility but no power. Wesleyan theology, however, needs to be more *biblical*.

Though a product of 1700s England when spiritual warfare was not a popular idea, Wesley had a surprising amount to say on this topic. Wesley notes that "It is God alone who can cast out Satan.

But he is generally pleased to do this by man . . . he chooses the weak to confound the mighty."[4] The mystery is that God can do this supernatural casting-out himself, but he prefers to use humans as the casting-out agents. Furthermore, it delights God to use his weaker people—the seemingly powerless—to be his agents of supernatural power.

Besides his sermon titled, "On Evil Angels"[5] in which Wesley explores the nature and properties of demonic forces, Wesley also wrote a sermon titled "A Caution Against Bigotry."[6] In this sermon, he asks the question why so few people cast out devils today. He says we should never forbid this to happen, and to welcome those who do. Wesley concludes his sermon by defining a *bigot* as a person who forbids others to cast out demons just because he or she has a personal preference to avoid this supernatural casting out of demons.

> We are not only to renounce evil, but to manifest truth. We tell people the world is vain; let our lives manifest that it is so. We tell them that our home is above and that all these things are transitory. Does our dwelling look like it? O to live consistent lives!
>
> Hudson Taylor

So how does this connect to social holiness? For this discussion, I want to look at casting out demons as confronting evil in all its forms. I have already mentioned the demonic power of prostitution that is alive in my community. For whatever reason, this destructive, enslaving practice seems to thrive in my area and to go largely unchecked by both Christians and non-Christians. Samaria is being skipped over. Then there is the demonic power of chemical addiction—this power that drags people down to practically nothing, until both body and soul are emaciated to the point of extinction. In my church alone we have had three suicide drug overdoses in the last year. When I see the power of hell wreaking this havoc, I know that we are not merely dealing with a person's willpower or a need to get a person to be more committed to Christ. This societal-level spiritual warfare requires that we maintain an unapologetic, unwavering faith in the goodness and imminence of God's kingdom. It requires that we be committed to holiness—both in our own personal selves, and to the belief that holiness is possible—that holiness *must* be possible—in our communities.

Jesus had a choice. While most Jews chose to take the bypass around Samaria Jesus chose to go through this land. His choice to go through Samaria was so shocking because Jews separated themselves from Samaritans. They refused to live in that neighborhood. And if they did, they certainly wouldn't walk through it. I'm sure you know the neighborhoods to which I am referring.

There are few demonic powers as insidious as the demonic power of segregation. Jews separated from Samaritans. The ethnic division was the obvious divider. But there were also divided worship styles, cultures, and beliefs. The one thing they had in common was their distaste for one another. Start resisting principalities and powers through prayer.

We have a man in our church named Nate. He's a quiet man—a wallflower. Nate has some mild mental illness and is a bit socially awkward. He always speaks slowly and quietly. In a crowd, he's easy to miss. But Nate has spiritual gifts of prayer and discernment. Many times this rather simple man will ask about a person or a situation at church, only to discover that the person or situation is in crisis and needs prayer. Nate comes in to the church many weekdays and every Sunday morning to sit in the prayer chapel and pray. He prays for church leadership, church finances, and people in crisis.

Few people would meet Nate and say, "Now here is a man of holy fire! Here is man who struggles against the principalities and powers!" And yet, this is exactly what Nate is. I believe that when Nate is sitting in that prayer chapel doing business with God, he is changing things on a supernatural and physical level.

Cast out those demonic powers of segregation! With unified prayer efforts, with political efforts, and with personal relationships—cast out those demonic powers of segregation. This must be an intentional act; it will not just happen. Casting out demons of any sort is not a natural work. We need supernatural acts to flow through God's people and spill out into our communities. If we are to be socially holy we must follow Jesus in acting against segregation by where we choose to live, to whom we reach out with the gospel, the style of music we use to worship, the language we use in our sermons, and the friendships we intentionally build. Does your church have a strong showing of Samaritans? Do you vote for the good of Samaritans? Do you have any deep friendships with Samaritans? Or are you tempted to skip Samaria?

Conclusion

Preaching. Healing. Casting out. Holiness is for so much more than personal purity. Holiness is also for power—power to make a difference in this world that we, in our natural states, cannot make. You can't preach? No problem. You can't heal society? No problem. You can't cast out society's demons? No problem. It's not about you anyway. It's about God and the work God wants to do through you.

Holiness itself has the idea of being distinct, different, set apart. But the purpose of this being set apart is not to segregate from society. The purpose is to engage. You see, holiness is not just a state of being. Holiness is designed to move us. And it's designed to move us to places like Samaria—places that might not have the romance of overseas mission trips. Places that might not have the safety or convenience of home. Places that you might, under normal circumstances, skip.

Following Jesus through and to Samaria will require supernatural power that you may not currently have. Following Jesus through Samaria will require power for preaching that probes the deepest wounds of society with conviction and abundant grace. Following Jesus through Samaria will require power to understand physical healing as a legitimate manifestation of God's kingdom. Following Jesus through Samaria will require power to represent our king in this earthly battle against the principalities and powers.

When will we go to Samaria? Or, a good question for The Wesleyan Church: When will we go *back* to Samaria?

The kingdom of God is strongest when we go through Samaria, learn from Samaria, and stay in Samaria.

Let's not skip Samaria!

We may never learn to love the smells of Samaria—the smell of homeless folks; the smell of sick, diseased people, even the smells of human waste and filth. But as we practice social holiness, we create new aromas. And the smell of redemption is always beautiful to those whom God has made holy.

"But thanks be to God, who always leads us in triumphal procession in Christ and through us spreads everywhere the fragrance of the knowledge of him. For we are to God the aroma of Christ among those who are being saved and those who are perishing. To the one we are the smell of death; to the other, the fragrance of life" (2 Cor. 2:14–16).

Questions for Personal Reflection and Application

1. How has this chapter illuminated your thinking about Jesus' command to go to Jerusalem, Judea, Samaria, and the far parts of the earth? How would you define your Samarias—the people or places you tend to skip?

2. What reasons do you see for being optimistic about the work that Jesus calls us to do in Samaria—preaching, healing, and casting out demons? What examples are you aware of where Christians have made a significant difference in their Samarias?

3. What might you or your congregation do to begin intentionally ministering in your Samarias or to minister more effectively or significantly?

Missional Holiness: Grace to Transform Our Communities

Executive Summary

Jesus told his followers to go to Jerusalem, Judea, Samaria, and the far parts of the earth. *Jerusalem* and *Judea* represented their homeland. The *far parts* were faraway places where people had different languages and cultures. Samaria was nearby, but a place that Jewish people tended to avoid. They looked down on Samaritans as unclean, unfaithful, and unholy. If they had a choice in the matter, they skipped Samaria. Yet Jesus does not give us a pass when it comes to ministering in our own Samarias—the places that we avoid going, if we can help it.

Jesus calls his followers to do three things in Samaria: preach, heal, and cast out demons.

Preaching to Samaria means recognizing spiritual powers at work in the structure of society and addressing these forces at a systemic level for God's kingdom. It is a dance between confrontation and grace—having the courage to bring up uncomfortable subjects, but doing it with the tenderness of the Savior, speaking words that restore dignity and hope.

Healing in Samaria involves introducing people to the Healer, Jesus, looking for ways we can be agents of healing in a diseased, sin-sick world. This includes addressing such problems as hazardous living conditions, health and nutrition concerns, and clean water.

Casting out demons in Samaria includes confronting evil in all of its forms, such as prostitution, drug abuse, ethnic segregation, and other areas where hell wreaks havoc.

Holiness is not just a state of being; it is designed to move us—to places like Samaria, places we might otherwise skip. Following Jesus to Samaria requires the supernatural power that is only available through the Holy Spirit.

JO ANNE LYON

Dr. Jo Anne Lyon is the founder of World Hope International, a Christ-centered relief and development organization, and served as its Chief Executive Officer until 2008. Through education, microenterprise, and community health, World Hope works in direct partnership with The Wesleyan Church and Wesleyans around the world to alleviate suffering and injustice. Dr. Lyon is an ordained minister in The Wesleyan Church and a Licensed Professional Counselor. She has been involved in urban, rural, and international development for more than forty years. In 2008, she was elected General Superintendent of The Wesleyan Church, the first woman to hold that office.

GLOBAL HOLINESS
Grace to Transform Our World

JO ANNE LYON

If we are going to make the world holy, we have to be personally holy. As N.T. Wright has said, "Personal holiness and global holiness belong together." Christy Lipscomb expressed this in such a wonderful way as she focused on holiness in the community. May her tribe increase! Now we want to focus on what this means regarding holiness in the world.

Holiness in the world is not a simple topic. As I wrapped my mind around it, though, I began to see that there are two elements of holiness that are necessary if we're going to be effective as God would have us be in the world, if we're going to experience lasting transformation personally and globally. We need to be pure in heart and we need power.

Pure in Heart

As believers, we cannot do anything significant in this world unless we are pure in heart. Jesus said, "Blessed are the pure in heart: for they shall see God" (Matt. 5:8 KJV). There is the initial cleansing we experience when the Holy Spirit comes in fullness, but as we *see* God, which is living in the immediate presence of God, he continues to reveal new things that bring repentance for more purity and more of the spirit. This is growth. John says it well: "But if we walk in the light, as he is in the light, we have fellowship with one another, and the blood of Jesus, his Son, purifies us from all sin (1 John 1:7).

Mildred Wynkoop expresses it another way in her book *Theology of Love*: "The coming of the Holy Spirit means the awakening of the total reserve of human nature. It is a honing of the sharp edge of human energies and capacities in order to fulfill one's God-appointed mission in life."[1] I have asked this question to many audiences: "Who would *not* want this?" This is the search that is set in our hearts at birth.

Steve Brown, a successful businessman and World Hope International board member, recently exemplified the practice of allowing God to shine light on his heart for further purity and being God's person in the global context. He writes in a recent publication of World Hope:

Though I come from a modest background and try to live a life that demonstrates my faith in Christ, it is all too easy for me to get caught up in the lies of self-importance that our society bestows upon people who have succeeded in business.

For my work, I travel internationally; I enjoy effortless transition from business class flights to five star hotels. Everyone seems eager to assist me and is very interested in what I say. I know this is an executive bubble and that there is a real world that isn't so comfortable. In fact, I know that the real word teems with people suffering absolute poverty. I also know that Christ has commanded that we share his compassion for the poor, to transform our thoughts and desires from ourselves to them. The question is, how can I make it not about me? How can I gain an understanding of the world in which the poor exist and to really make a difference for them?[2]

As we walk with God and he is constantly purifying us, we begin to have his eyes and to see things around us differently. He begins to change our desires.

In 1985, I was invited to accompany an ABC News team to Ethiopia during the severe famine. It was one of the first times we in America began to see all these heartbreaking visions and images of hunger and starvation piped into our living rooms.

Frankly, I was absolutely overwhelmed. I had never seen so many people in one place experiencing such incredible suffering. The stories abounded of entire families trying to make it to the feeding camps but burying half the family, both young and old, on the journey. My unconscious response of not fully embracing the suffering was to hang out with the film crew, supposedly being a help to them.

> He has showed you, O man, what is good. And what does the LORD require of you? To act justly and to love mercy and to walk humbly with your God.
>
> Micah 6:8

After a few days, we traveled to one of the most desperate places, the name Korem, where the feeding camp had 250,000 people. It was here that a nurse from Save the Children United Kingdom grabbed my hand and said, "Jo Anne, I'm taking you out to the field." I had no recourse but to follow her. The field is where people coming to the camp for help first enter. Several times daily, health professionals go out to the field and determine the level of need and make the assignments as to what section of the feeding camps they will work next.

When we walked out to the field, I realized there were thousands of people sitting totally silent. "Why are they so quiet?" I asked the nurse.

Her response still rings in my ears. "Because they are conserving every breath they have. Every breath is a calorie."

As I saw that mass of people that day—hungry, starving, dying—I prayed, "Lord, don't let me ever see people through my own eyes again. Please help me to see them through your eyes from this day forward." He has answered that prayer. There are times when I haven't *wanted* to see people through his eyes. But I want to tell you, he will help you begin to see the world through his eyes, and it transforms everything about you.

> But just as he who called you is holy, so be holy in all you do; for it is written: "Be holy, because I am holy.
>
> 1 Peter 1:15

Perhaps one of the reasons preaching and teaching on heart purity has declined in the last quarter century has been some of the unfortunate by-products of holiness teaching. One of these is the trap of obsessive introspection, resulting in paralysis of action. E. Stanley Jones used to refer to it as *paralysis of analysis*. Others have established criteria beyond scripture of what heart purity looks like, thereby resulting in legalism and judgmentalism.

A recent by-product regarding heart purity has been extensive teaching on sexual purity, marriage fidelity, and many other subjects. But this type of purity cannot exist without heart purity. Through World Hope and The Wesleyan Church, we are deeply involved in the HIV/AIDS crisis. In the teaching of HIV/AIDS prevention and lifestyle changes, we have found that some thirty-five thousand young people in Southern Africa are now saying, "This is more than just abstaining from sex outside of marriage—we want to live holy lives." We believe this is a Holiness revival happening in the midst of the pain and suffering of HIV/AIDS.

At Pentecost, images of fire reflected the deep cleansing that took place—the new life that was formed—the beginning of the church. God's people gathered! And it's my prayer in our Church today that God will continue to keep us cleansed. And do you know what that also means? It means repentance, all along the way. That's how we continue to stay pure.

Holiness Is Power for Redemption Personally and Globally

If power is not connected with heart purity, there is disaster personally and for entire nations. We have many examples in scripture, history, and contemporary society, both within the church and outside it. This is the only way we can experience the results of Jesus' prayer: "My prayer is not that you take them out of the world, but that you protect them from the evil one" (John 17:15).

For years, I struggled with something Jesus said to his disciples, and I think I'm finally getting it. Remarkably, Jesus told his disciples, ". . . anyone who has faith in me will do what I have been doing. He will do even greater things than these, because I am going to the Father" (John 14:12). He's going to the Father and sending us the Holy Spirit and literally, greater things will we do than Jesus did. Think about the Apostle Peter. Prior to Pentecost, Peter was paralyzed in his starts and stops. Peter preaching at Pentecost with boldness and courage is a specific fulfillment of the prophetic words Jesus spoke to his disciples.

A few months ago, I had a call from a *Washington Times* reporter. He said, "I'm going with President Bush to Africa and someone told me I should call you. What do you think about aid to Africa?" I gave him my thoughts and we had an excellent conversation.

A few days later, the same reporter phoned me again. This time, he was at the airport on his way to Africa. He said, "You know, you said some things the other day when we talked. I was in the car, and I wasn't able to write everything down." So I tried to repeat some of the things I had said a few days earlier. Then a surprise question came at the conclusion. "Jo Anne, why do you do what you do?"

It was an interesting opportunity, and I thought, *"You know what? I'm going to go for the whole enchilada. I don't care what he's going to write in the newspaper."* I ventured into the conversation, "Well, you know, before Jesus left this earth, he said, 'As the Father has sent me, I am sending you' (John 20:21, emphasis added). 'As' refers to all the things that Jesus did. So I'm just trying to do all the things that Jesus did. That's what all of us are doing." And then I thought, *"You know what? I'm going to go a bit further here."* I said, "And Jesus said, 'Greater things will you do because I go to the Father' (John 14:12 paraphrased). When he went to the Father, Jesus sent the Holy Spirit. We really can't do it without the power of the Holy Spirit."

The phone was just dead on the other end. I thought, *"This guy is thinking, 'This woman is wacky.'"*

And then I heard this faint voice, and he said, "Wow! Jo Anne, will you pray for me while I'm in Africa?" That's what this world is looking for: the real power of the Holy Spirit.

Jesus' message was not about establishing a theocratic Christendom. It was a different kind of revolution, in which the power of God is demonstrated through weakness, love, healing, forgiveness, and reconciliation. The kingdom operates subversively and sacrificially—not through power and prestige.

In John Wesley's sermon entitled "The Way of Salvation,"[3] he states that justification leads naturally and necessarily in this life to sanctification—to doing justly, loving mercy, and walking humbly with God (Mic. 6:8). Sanctification has corporate and social dimensions, thereby becoming part of the church with a mission to overcome the unholiness, alienation, and hopelessness of the present world.

> Sanctify them by the truth; your word is truth. As you sent me into the world, I have sent them into the world. For them I sanctify myself, that they may be truly sanctified.
>
> John 17:17–19

However, I believe we as Wesleyans have some repentance to do in this dimension. The merging General Conference of The Wesleyan Church in 1968, reflects this need. During that year the world was experiencing significant social crises – Martin Luther King, Jr. had been murdered, Robert Kennedy had been murdered, Africa was emerging from colonialism and all the issues that arose with that. Radical Liberation Theology was making its statements of revolution in Latin America. The Cold War was dividing the world. Cities in the U.S. burned. Racism was flagrant. We were tangled in an unpopular war in Southeast Asia. Youth were desperately turning to drugs because of hopelessness. Dangerous nuclear build-up was beginning, and much, much more could be added to the list.

Yet, at our merging conference we were buried in our constitutions and made no reference to the world around us. Before his recent death, Dr. Virgil Mitchell, Church Statesman and former General

Superintendent was challenged by this omission from a student doing research. Dr. Mitchell in his ever learning spirit recognized the omission and said with great passion, " May God forgive us and may we never be that removed from society again."

The twenty-first-century world desperately needs purity and power—the hope of life *before death*—God's future kingdom invading the present. Wesley emphasized that the Holy Spirit is the bond of unity in the church—as we draw near to God, we draw near to one another, resulting in God's sanctifying love that moves us out to the world.

Many times God's power looks impotent in the face of worldly power. But the power of God works in a totally different realm. Nearly two decades ago we witnessed the fall of the Berlin Wall, symbolizing freedom to millions of oppressed. A few years prior to this time, an acquaintance of mine visited Moscow and went to one of the large ornate Russian Orthodox churches, where he joined five *babushkas*, older women. They were praying, and they were the only ones in this cavernous building. Their wrinkled skin reflected the difficult life they were experiencing. This visitor asked them why they were even bothering to come to pray with the resistance all around. With cheerful spirits they responded, "We believe in a God who has power to deliver us from evil."

> I believe the holier a man becomes, the more he mourns over the unholiness which remains in him
>
> C.H. Spurgeon

The man continued to pray with them, but as he left and made his way to Red Square, he couldn't help but feel that their praying seemed hopeless. The display of all that worldly power overwhelmed him to the point that any thread of faith and hope he had vanished. Then he sensed God almost laughing and saying to him,

"Don't you think I have the power to deliver these people through five old women?" And we've seen the results.

We have all admired William Wilberforce and Hannah Moore for their courage to fight the slave trade. They are excellent models of purity and the power of God to overcome evil and oppression.

Today billions are crying for release from evil.

I believe one of the most difficult areas in our global community in which to overcome evil is that of *consumerism* and *selfishness*, fulfilling personal pleasure and gain at any cost.

We see this resulting in:

- 1.1 billion people who have never heard the name of Jesus;
- human trafficking, with twenty-seven million slaves in the world today;
- rebel wars;
- economic inequities, with three billion people living on less than two dollars a day (recently World Bank President Robert Zoellick said, "While many are worrying about filling their gas tanks, many others around the world are struggling to fill their stomachs." This should be very sobering to us.);
- abortion;
- same sex marriage;
- HIV/AIDS, with fourteen million AIDS orphans;
- Racism;
- Tribalism;
- pornography in all its forms—print, internet, and film;
- domestic violence;
- drug and alcohol abuse;
- and the list goes on.

Recently, there have been books and articles written by policy people regarding the need for the church to intervene in these issues. The secular intellectuals of our world are seeing something that is beyond their comprehension, but also represents a hope they are ready to engage. Walter Russell Meade, senior fellow at the Council on Foreign Relations, wrote a compelling article in the September 2006 *Foreign Affairs Journal*.[4] In the article, he argues that thoughtful Evangelicals are "likely to provide something now sadly lacking in the world of U.S. foreign policy." The reason, he says, is that Evangelicals realize we are in a fallen world and yet have optimism for redemption. When this kind of statement comes from a liberal think tank, is that not an open door for us to walk through and bring healing and holiness to this world? Would not the power of holiness with pure hearts be welcomed at these tables?

In days gone by, the power of holiness lived out in God's people, has been at the tables of power as well as in the streets. It was said of Catherine Booth that she lobbied Queen Victoria on behalf of the poor and would also walk the streets with the poor. That's the kind of thing we're talking about.

The resurrection of Jesus is the beginning of the new creation, of victory over sin and death, and it continues through us. Jesus' resurrection calls us to dangerous and difficult tasks on earth. The power of holiness gives us the necessary tools for the task. We cannot leave the world as it is and allow evil to proceed unchecked.

But most of us will excuse ourselves from plunging into the world equipped with purity and power. Often we allow excuses like a lack of education or influence to keep us from following our God appointed mission in life, both personally and corporately. These same excuses are sometimes used in The Wesleyan Church corporately as well.

But Srey Mon of Cambodia defies the excuses. At fifteen years of age, she was married in a village community in Cambodia. Having never had the opportunity to attend school, she was illiterate, as were 80 percent of the rural women in Cambodia.

One day Srey Mon's husband said to her, "I'm going to take you to the city." She had never been to the city before, so she was excited to go. When they arrived in the city, they checked in at the guest house. She went to the room, and her husband informed her he would be there soon.

She waited. One hour. Two hours. Finally, she went to the owner of the guest house and asked, "Where is my husband?"

The owner of the guest house laughed and said, "Oh, you're husband is gone. This is not a guest house. This is a brothel, and your husband has just sold you to me for two hundred dollars. I now own you."

She suffered intensely for four years in that brothel, experiencing electric shock and starvation when she did not obey. She was made to service fifteen to twenty customers every day. Raised a Buddhist, Srey said, "I was looking for the real God."

> There is no shortcut to holiness; it must be the business of our whole lives.
>
> William Wilberforce

One night, miraculously, she escaped. It's a miracle, because generally they have those brothels cemented in the back. You can only get in and out through the front. She made her way to a home that World Hope International works with in Cambodia. There she was welcomed and loved for who she was, and it wasn't long until she did find the real God. She found him, and I have never met anyone who loved him more intensely.

Two years after Srey had been able to escape, I visited Cambodia. Srey Mon was trying to teach me how to spin cotton and weave a rug. To do this spinning, you have to sit on a can that is six inches high. I kept falling off! Srey would put her hand over on my hand and laugh. Then I realized her hand was very warm. As I looked into her very bony face, the light of Jesus shone brightly. You see, she was only fifty-eight pounds, dying of AIDS.

The staff shared with me that they had taken her to the doctor the week before to assist her in her dying, to make her more comfortable. After the examination, she looked up at the Buddhist doctor and said, "I love Jesus with all my heart!" That day the Buddhist doctor put his head on her tiny little shoulder and started crying. He said, "I want to know your Jesus." My friends, that's holiness purity and power.

> Give me one hundred preachers who fear nothing but sin and desire nothing but God, and I care not whether they be clergymen or laymen, they alone will shake the gates of Hell and set up the kingdom of Heaven upon Earth.
>
> John Wesley

On that same trip, I received a call from the U.S. Embassy in Cambodia. They said, "The ambassador from the State Department is here and he'd like to have breakfast with you."

I said, "Yes, may I bring some folks from some of the other agencies along?" They agreed. So I contacted all the faith-based groups in Cambodia, working in this dark field of human trafficking. We had a wonderful breakfast.

The ambassador decided he would like to visit some of the groups in the field. One of the groups he chose to visit was the home where Srey Mon happened to be living. After the warm welcome from the women in the home, he asked if he could hear some of the stories of the women. It is necessary to preserve the women's dignity, therefore their personal stories are handled with respect. So we arranged a room for them to visit. One of the stories he heard was Srey's story.

Later, as we walked out, he had tears rolling down his face. He said, "Her story *really* impacted me." I found this quite interesting since her story, horrible as it is, did not involve the same kinds of unspeakable torture as some of the other stories.

Two months later, Srey went to be with Jesus. I called the ambassador and said, "Ambassador, I just wanted to let you know that Srey passed away."

He was totally silent on the other end. Then he said, "She *really* impacted me."

Jesus uses the unlikely, the un-powerful.

Two months later, I received a call from the State Department on a Sunday night with a curious request, "Jo Anne, we're having a big event at the State Department. It's a salute to the twenty-first-century abolitionists." I had already been invited, and I was planning to go. The group making the final plans said, "Secretary of State Condoleezza Rice is going to speak, as well as two Congressmen who have been very supportive of the legislation regarding human trafficking, and the Ambassador will bring the final speech. We think we need a prayer. Would you be willing to come and pray prior to the Secretary's speech?"

I agreed. So two days later, I made my way to the State Department in the Benjamin Franklin Room with hundreds of people present, including many cabinet members as well as the diplomatic staff. I prayed the prayer, Secretary Rice gave a compelling speech, and the congress people gave short speeches identifying this twenty-first-century issue as far larger than the nineteenth-century issue. The Ambassador of the Trafficking in Persons Office of the State Department reviewed the countries he'd visited and the policies that had been enacted to try to put an end to human trafficking. Then my ears perked up as he started saying, "But you know, the person that influenced me the most. Her name is Srey Mon in Cambodia." I wanted to fall out of that chair. I couldn't believe it. He then told her story and tried to explain why she had influenced him so much. But he could not quite explain it fully. I secretly wanted to jump out of my chair and finish the story for him.

Srey's story impacted the Ambassador, the doctor, and all of us because of her purity of heart and love for Jesus—one young woman, filled with the spirit of God and holiness, impacting the greatest earthly powers.

That's our God at work in the world today and he wants to use anyone who will seek after a pure heart and follow God in holiness.

May it be said of The Wesleyan Church of the twenty-first century—they plunged into the world, restoring God's kingdom and were kept from the evil one. God bless you.

Questions for Personal Reflection and Application

1. What do you think it means to take holiness to the world? What are your thoughts about the statement that personal holiness and global holiness belong together?

2. This chapter states that believers are not able to do anything significant in the world without being pure in heart. Do you agree or disagree? What difference should this make in our personal lives? What difference should it make in the life of our congregation?

3. This chapter states that the power of the Holy Spirit is essential for transforming our world, personally and globally. What can you do specifically this week to seek the empowerment of the Holy Spirit for you personally and for your congregation?

Global Holiness:
Grace to Transform Our World

Executive Summary

To make the world holy, we must be personally holy. If we're going to experience lasting transformation personally and globally, we need to be *pure in heart* and we need *power*.

Being pure in heart requires repentance. Christians experience an initial cleansing when the Holy Spirit comes in fullness, but as we live in the immediate presence of God, he continues to reveal new things that bring repentance for more purity and more of the spirit. There must be growth in purity after the initial cleansing. Unfortunately, many Christians have thought that purity can be reduced to rule keeping and legalism. Instead it is a deep desire to live a holy life.

In addition to purity of heart, we need power to transform the world. Holiness is power for redemption both personally and globally. Jesus told his disciples that after he went away he would send the Holy Spirit and that they (and we) would do greater things than he had done. As we try to take holiness to the world we need the power of the Holy Spirit, but power must be connected with purity or there will be trouble. Jesus' message was about a different kind of revolution in which the power of God is demonstrated through weakness, love, healing, forgiveness, and reconciliation. The kingdom operates subversively and sacrificially—not through wordly power and prestige.

The twenty-first century desperately needs purity and power—the hope of life before death—God's future kingdom invading the present. The resurrection of Jesus is the beginning of the new creation and it continues through us. We cannot leave the world as it is and allow evil to proceed unchecked. The power of holiness gives us the necessary tools for the task.

NOTES

Chapter 1—Personal Holiness: Grace for Transformed Lives

1. Keith Drury, *Holiness for Ordinary People* (Indianapolis, Ind.: Wesleyan Publishing House, 1994), 71–88.

2. Kenneth Grider, *A Wesleyan-Holiness Theology* (Kansas City, Mo.: Beacon Hill, 1994), 367–468.

3. "Article of Religion XIV: Sanctification: Initial, Progressive, Entire," *The Discipline of the Wesleyan Church 2000* (Indianapolis, Ind.: Wesleyan Publishing House, 2000), 238.

4. Steve DeNeff, *Whatever Became of Holiness?* (Indianapolis, Ind.: Wesleyan Publishing House, 1996), 125–137.

5. John Wesley, "The Scripture Way of Salvation," *The Works of John Wesley* (Kansas City, Mo.: Beacon Hill, 1979), VI: 43–54.

6. See note 3 above.

7. Thomas Oden, *Systematic Theology*, vol. 3, *Life in the Spirit* (San Francisco, Calif.: HarperCollins, 1994), 226–257.

8. Randy Maddox, *Responsible Grace: John Wesley's Practical Theology* (Nashville, Tenn.: Kingswood, 1994), 176–190.

9. John Wesley, "Brief Thoughts on Christian Perfection," *The Works of John Wesley* (Kansas City, Mo.: Beacon Hill, 1979), XI: 446.

10. John Wesley, "Farther Thoughts on Christian Perfection," *The Works of John Wesley* (Kansas City, Mo.: Beacon Hill, 1979), XI: 414–427.

11. DeNeff, *Whatever Became of Holiness,* 141–150.

12. Drury, *Holiness for Ordinary People*, 89–95.

13. John Wesley, "Plain Account of Christian Perfection," *The Works of John Wesley* (Kansas City, Mo.: Beacon Hill, 1979), XI: 443.

14. John Wesley, "Causes for the Inefficacy of Christianity," *The Works of John Wesley*, (Kansas City, Mo.: Beacon Hill, 1979), VII: 281–290.

15. I am indebted to Dr. Keith Drury for his thorough reading of a preliminary draft of this chapter that resulted in constructive comments integrated into the body of the chapter.

Chapter 2—Corporate Holiness: Grace to Transform Our Churches

1. On November 4, 2008, voters in the state of California approved Proposition 8 by 52.1 percent. On November 19, 2008, the California Supreme Court voted six to one to hear and review legal challenges to Proposition 8. The court refused to grant a stay that would have permitted gay marriages to resume pending their decision. The court had not yet begun hearing arguments as this book went to press.

2. On November 2, 2008, more than 33,000 people gathered at Qualcomm Stadium. Public, corporate prayer continued for twelve hours.

3. Donald W. Dayton, *Discovering an Evangelical Heritage* (New York: Harper and Row, 1976).

4. As of this writing, Carol is in remission, for which we praise God.

Chapter 3—Missional Holiness: Grace to Transform Our Communities

1. John Wesley, "An Extract of the Rev. Mr. John Wesley's Journal," *The Works of John Wesley* (Kansas City, Mo.: Beacon Hill, 1979), IV: 311.

2. John Wesley, "An Extract of the Rev. Mr. John Wesley's Journal," *The Works of John Wesley* (Kansas City, Mo.: Beacon Hill, 1979), I: 406.

3. Robert G. Tuttle, "John Wesley and the Gifts of the Holy Spirit," http://www.goodnewsmag.org/library/articles/tuttle-so96.htm, accessed 12/08/08.

4. John Wesley, "A Caution Against Bigotry," *The Works of John Wesley* (Kansas City, Mo.: Beacon Hill, 1979), V: 483.

5. John Wesley, "On Evil Angels," *The Works of John Wesley* (Kansas City, Mo.: Beacon Hill, 1979), VI: 370–380.

6. John Wesley, "A Caution Against Bigotry," *The Works of John Wesley* (Kansas City, Mo.: Beacon Hill, 1979), V: 479–492.

Chapter 4—Global Holiness: God's Grace to Transform Our World

1. Mildred Wynkoop, *Theology of Love*, (Kansas City, Mo.: Beacon Hill, 1972).

2. Steve Brown, "Participating in WHI's Economic Development Initiatives," World Hope Live 12, no.2 (2008): 8.

3. John Wesley, "The Scripture Way of Salvation," *The Works of John Wesley* (Kansas City, Mo.: Beacon Hill, 1979), VI: 43–54.

4. Walter Russell Mead, "God's Country?" Foreign Affairs 85, no. 5 (2006), http://www.foreignaffairs.org/20060901faessay85504/walter-russell-mead/god-s-country.html.

QUESTIONS FOR GROUP DISCUSSION

Chapter 1—Personal Holiness: Grace for Transformed Lives

1. How much importance do the Christians you know place on personal holiness?

2. Would you say that interest in personal holiness is increasing or decreasing in the church today? What are the reasons for your answer?

3. Do you think people in the church or more optimistic or pessimistic regarding the possibility of entire sanctification? What are the reasons for your answer?

4. Do you see any differences between generations in belief, attitudes, or approaches to personal holiness?

5. What are some of the negative attitudes or outcomes that you have seen connected with the teaching of holiness in the church? What are the most positive attitudes or outcomes you have seen?

6. How have you seen the teaching of The Wesleyan Church changing on the topic of holiness?

7. How can the local church best help and support Christians who want to live holy lives?

8. Dr. Bounds says, "The beauty of The Wesleyan Church's teaching is the optimism and expectation that God can work in the present moment to bring about entire sanctification." How have you seen such optimism displayed in the church? How can the church encourage such optimism?

9. Based on your own experience with seeking entire sanctification, what do you think of the spiritual counsel Dr. Bounds offers on experiencing entire sanctification? What would you add or take away?

10. What is the single most important teaching that you are taking away from the presentation on personal holiness? How will it make a difference in your life?

Chapter 2—Corporate Holiness: Grace to Transform Our Churches

1. Before reading this chapter, how familiar were you with the topic of corporate holiness? How much or little has it been emphasized in the congregations to which you've belonged?

2. Have you ever personally experienced what Dr. Garlow describes as *atmospheric holiness*? Tell the group about your experience.

3. How much is corporate holiness something we cultivate and how much is it something God simply decides to grant? How would you describe what we can do and what God alone can do regarding corporate holiness?

4. Discuss the following statement by Dr. Garlow: "If individuals are able to make choices that create an environment where God's grace is released in personal holiness, congregations can also make choices that create an environment in which God's grace is released in corporate or atmospheric holiness." What do you think is the significance of that statement?

5. Why do you think that *brokenness* is such a key aspect of corporate holiness? Have you ever been involved in a congregation that experienced such corporate brokenness? Tell the group about your experience.

6. Do you agree that the desperation of the church is a means for God to offer the grace of corporate holiness? What are some areas where you think the church is or should be feeling a sense of desperation?

7. Does your congregation make use of any kind of formal liturgy, such as reciting creeds? What effects or benefits have you seen in your church from including such elements in worship?

8. What are some key areas where your congregation and its members need to simplify? How do you think the act of simplifying in those areas would benefit the congregation and its sense of corporate holiness?

9. Is corporate holiness God's plan for the church? Are you convinced that corporate holiness is a reality that is distinct from personal holiness? Why or why not?

10. What is the single most important teaching you will take away from the presentation on corporate holiness? How do you think it can make a difference in your church's life?

Chapter 3—Missional Holiness: Grace to Transform Our Communities

1. What is your church's Samaria? List several possible answers to the question and describe them all in detail.

2. How well is your congregation doing in ministering to its Samaria?

3. What would it take for your congregation to effectively minister in its Samaria?

4. What are the challenges and obstacles that you see to your congregation ministering to its Samaria? How might your church overcome the obstacles?

5. How can a congregation empower people to minister within their own personal Samaria?

6. What message or messages do you think need to be preached in your congregation's Samaria?

7. How might your congregation preach the truth with kindness, care, and compassion in its Samaria?

8. Where does your congregation's Samaria need healing? What are its sicknesses? How might your congregation promote the health of people and society in your congregation's Samaria? What other congregations or agencies might your congregation partner with to promote health and healing in your congregation's Samaria?

9. What evils need to be cast out of your congregation's Samaria? What practical, tangible steps might your congregation be able to take to begin addressing some of those evils? What other congregations or agencies might your congregation partner with to cast out demons in its Samaria?

10. What is the single most important teaching you will take away from the presentation on missional holiness in our communities? How do you think it can make a difference for you, your church, and your community?

Chapter 4—Global Holiness: Grace to Transform Our World

1. Discuss the quote by N.T. Wright: "Personal holiness and global holiness belong together." What are the implications for Christians and the church?

2. Why do you think purity of heart is an essential aspect of missional holiness?

3. Have you ever had an experience where you felt as though you were seeing people through God's eyes? How did the experience impact or change you?

4. How do you think it would change the church and the world if Christians were to see the world through God's eyes? What differences would it make in the attitudes and behaviors of God's people?

5. Do you agree that preaching and teaching about heart purity have declined in the last twenty-five years? What do you think are the reasons?

6. What do you think it means that holiness is power for redemption personally and globally? What examples can you give from your own experience or the experience of others?

7. Dr. Lyon says that if power is not connected with heart purity, there's trouble. Do you agree or disagree? What kind of trouble might it cause?

8. Discuss this statement from the chapter: "Jesus' message was not about establishing a theocratic Christendom. It was a different kind of revolution, in which the power of God is demonstrated through weakness, love, healing, forgiveness, and reconciliation. The kingdom operates subversively and sacrificially—not through power and prestige." What are the implications for the church?

9. Discuss this statement from the chapter: "The twenty-first century world desperately needs purity and power—the hope of life before death—God's future kingdom invading the present." How can the church be a part making this a reality?

10. What is the single most important teaching you will take away from the presentation on mission holiness in our world? How do you think it can make a difference for you, your church, and your world?

Also on Holiness from Wesleyan Publishing House

Be Holy: God's Invitation to Understand, Declare, and Experience Holiness edited by Joseph Coleson
ISBN: 978-0-89827-372-4

Holiness for Ordinary People by Keith Drury
ISBN: 978-0-89827-278-9

Holy and Human: Overcoming Spiritual Struggles to Live a Holy Life by Earle L. Wilson
ISBN: 978-0-89827-355-7

More than Forgiveness: What Jesus Wants You to Know About the Holy Life by Steve DeNeff
ISBN: 978-0-89827-244-4

The Way Forward: Discovering the Classic Message of Holiness edited by Jeremy Summers and Matt LeRoy
ISBN: 978-0-89827-356-4

Whatever Became of Holiness? by Steve DeNeff
ISBN: 978-0-89827-156-8

www.wesleyan.org/wph

HOLINESS

DISCOVER THE POWER THAT CAN TRANSFORM YOU YOUR CHURCH, AND YOUR WORLD

- **What is holiness?**
- **What does it mean to live a holy life?**
- **Can an ordinary person aspire to be holy?**

In this practical, highly readable book, you will discover the meaning of holiness and be inspired to seek this life-transforming experience for yourself. A unique panel of experts, including a theologian, a megachurch pastor, an inner-city pastor, and a national church leader, explain the power of holiness in everyday language. This brief, challenging book will inspire you to believe in the promise behind God's command to "Be holy for I am holy" as you both understand and experience holiness as never before.

Each chapter includes questions for reflection and application, and a brief discussion guide will enable you to explore this exciting teaching with others.

wph wesleyan publishing house
Indianapolis, Indiana

For other life-changing books, visit us at
www.wesleyan.org/wph

RELIGION / Christian Life / Spiritual Growth
ISBN: 978-0-89827-409-7

90000

9 780898 274097